Activities Deskbook

for teaching reading skills

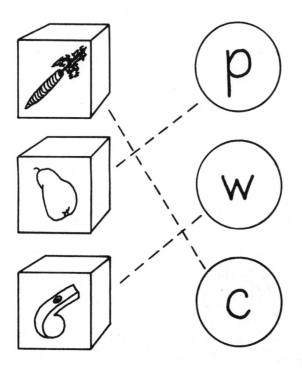

Activities Deskbook

for teaching reading skills

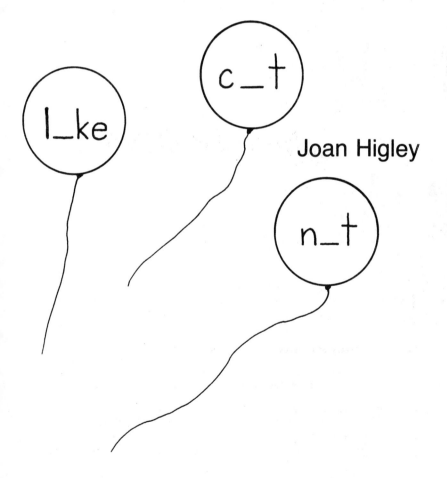

Joan Higley

Parker Publishing Company, Inc.   West Nyack, N.Y.

© 1977, by

PARKER PUBLISHING COMPANY, INC.

West Nyack, N.Y.

Sixth Printing . . . . . July, 1979

Library of Congress Cataloging in Publication Data

Higley, Joan,
    Activities deskbook for teaching reading skills.

    1. Reading (Elementary)--Handbooks, manuals, etc.
2. Creative activities and seat work--Handbooks,
manuals, etc. I. Title.
LB1050.2.H53   372.4'1   76-54643
ISBN 0-13-003541-6

Printed in the United States of America

to my loving husband David
and my daughter JJ

practical value
this book
offers educators

This book, and the many innovative ideas it contains, is written to supplement standard reading programs by stimulating teacher effectiveness and pupil interest.

This exceptionally practical manual describes a broad range of techniques, activities and time-tested ideas that can be used to modernize your reading courses, excite student interest in acquiring correct reading habits and improve reading aptitude.

Reading ability is the mastery of many skills. For example, the student must learn and appreciate rules and skills relating to structural analysis, vocabulary development, visual/auditory discrimination and recognition, etc. This book covers *all* the basic reading skills, each with a number of supplementary ideas that are brief, to the point, easily understood and simply implemented. The techniques and activities are all "teacher tested," and they have been used extensively in the author's reading classes. Moreover, since good reading habits are acquired by sensory experience, the visual aspects of reading are supplemented with speech, touch and auditory appreciation.

As an example of what you will find in this book, the following can be used to explain *contractions*:

Short-Cut Words

purpose: to introduce the concept of contractions
materials: chalkboard and chalk
procedure:
   1. The teacher produces the following display on the board:

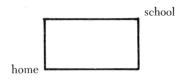

2. The teacher tells the children the following story:

There once was a man who had a field where he grew corn. During the summer no one was allowed to cross the field, so the people had to go the long way around.

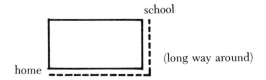

But in the winter, snow covered the frozen ground and people were able to take a shortcut.

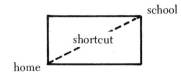

3. The same story is applied to contractions:

Sometimes we use the long way around, and sometimes we use the shortcut to say or write the same thought:

   You will find that the boys and girls learn much faster if they are able to see the concept as it is explained to them.

   This book is full of brief, to-the-point creative ideas that you can use to supplement your basic reading program. The materials it offers can be used for individualized instruction, small group work and for teaching the class as a whole. In all, this work contains some 250 illustrated reading activities and 20 additional miscellaneous techniques to stimulate pupil interest, imagination and progress. Structured from the simple to the more difficult, these materials are organized into 12 chapters according to subject content and reading skill. The activities are all accompanied by step-by-step instructions, and most of the activities can be made self-checking to save you valuable classroom time. The necessary materials are generally those found in the classroom—there is little or no requirement that your school or you purchase items that are often overpriced and seldom used. Finally, as you have noticed, this manual is bound in a way that permits the pages to be laid flat both for easy reading and reproduction of the numerous worksheets accompanying the activities.

You may agree that "variety is the spice of life," and this book will help you add variety to your reading program. It will also do much more. The materials that follow will assist you in your efforts to make reading one of the most interesting, enjoyable and stimulating experiences for your students. Moreover, since these practical ideas can be important stepping stones to further creative thought, your imagination will be stimulated and the "teaching experience" more fully enjoyed. Above all, these materials will make your reading program more enjoyable—and more effective.

Joan Higley

contents

2   Motor Response Reading Activities   37

3   Picture Clues for Reading Reinforcement   53

4   Unlocking Meanings with Context Clues   75

5 Strengthening Recall Abilities 91

6   Auditory Perception: Identifying Similar Sounds   101

7   Auditory Discrimination: Hearing Differences in Sounds   113

8   Visual Recognition Activities   123

11   Structural Analysis: The Basics of Word Forms and Variations

Plurals

Prefixes and Suffixes

Syllables

Compound Words

Contractions

Homonymns, Antonymns and Synonyms

12   Activities to Stimulate Pupil Interest and Creativity   217

1   oral response reading activities

Effective reading originates with effective listening. Thus, the materials that follow begin with activities that require the student to "listen and identify," "listen and respond," or "listen and classify," etc.

Moreover, this chapter aids the student in developing his or her ability to follow directions, identify, classify, organize sequentially, associate and repeat. The activities generally require an oral response by the child and thus are classified as "oral response reading activities"; occasionally, the child may be permitted to explain his or her answer by art form, thus providing for variation in response.

Finally, the chapter contains follow-up worksheets to reinforce oral skills. These materials are very useful for young readers and provide the teacher with concept-introducing activities.

How Many?

purpose: to listen to and identify how many words the teacher uses
materials: an oral or written activity; wax paper and Cool Whip
procedure:

1. The teacher reads a simple sentence.

   Example: See the cat.

2. The child listens and keeps track of how many words there are in the sentence.

   Example: See the cat=3.

3. The child responds by saying, "Three."

4. The same activity can be done by giving each child a piece of wax paper and a dab of Cool Whip.

5. The child responds by writing "3" with the Cool Whip on wax paper.

6. The teacher can work toward reading longer sentences.

Listen and Do

purpose: to listen and respond
materials: an oral or written activity; paper and pencil
procedure:

1.   The teacher gives a series of three numbers (e.g., 6, 5, 1) and the child repeats them orally or writes them on paper. After many 3-number combinations have been given, the teacher can increase the activity to 4 and 5 number combinations.

2.   The teacher can use letters instead of numbers (e.g., A, A, B; A, D, C, D).

3.   The teacher can use words in categories that the child has to repeat orally or draw on paper.

   Example: Apple, peach, orange

variation: have the child reverse the order.

   Example: The teacher says, "6, 5, 1."
   The child says, "1, 5, 6."

Follow Me

purpose: to listen to and follow directions
materials: an oral or a drawn activity; paper and crayons
procedure:

1.   The teacher gives a direction and the child listens and does the activity.

   Example: Go to the door.

2.   The directions may increase and the child does the activity after all directions have been given.

   Example: Go to the sink.
   Turn the water on.
   Turn the water off.
   Walk backward to your desk.

3.   The same activity can be done as a drawn activity. The teacher gives a directed statement and the child responds.

   Example: Draw a house.

4.   The directions may become more extensive and the child listens and follows after all directions have been given.

   Example: Draw a house.
   Draw a tree next to the house.
   Draw a cat in the tree.

Word Fun

purpose: to listen to and orally associate related words
materials: an oral activity
procedure:
1. The teacher mentions a key word (e.g., *apple*).
2. The first child thinks of another word suggested by the key word (e.g., *fruit*). The child does not have to repeat the key word.
3. The next child continues the game by mentioning another related word (e.g., *seeds*).
4. After approximately 5 or 6 words have been mentioned, the next child repeats *all* words that have been said in order—or in reverse order.

What's Your Category?

purpose: to listen and be able to classify orally
materials: an oral activity
procedure:
1. The teacher mentions a category of items.

   Example: Robin, jay, wren, sparrow.

2. The child listens carefully and decides what the category is and says the category orally.

   Example: robin, jay, wren, sparrow—birds.

3. Some further suggestions for categories are as follows:

   tulip, rose, daisy—flowers
   red, blue, green—colors
   round, square, triangle—shapes
   dog, cat, bird—pets
   coat, dress, pants—clothes
   chair, table, bed—furniture
   New York, Washington, Los Angeles—cities

Put in Order

purpose: to provide practice in sequencing
materials: an oral activity; plain paper, scissors, paste and worksheet (See page 28.)
procedure:
1. The teacher reads a group of 3 phrases.

   Example: Eat breakfast.

Worksheet

Eat breakfast

Get out of bed

Get dressed

Get out of bed.
Get dressed.

2. The child listens and orally repeats the 3 phrases in their proper sequence.

Example: Get out of bed.
Get dressed.
Eat breakfast.

3. The child then is given a follow-up worksheet from which he or she is to cut out the pictures and paste them in their proper order on a plain sheet of paper.

Yes-Yes

purpose: to listen to and orally identify like sounds
materials: an oral activity
procedures:
1. The teacher mentions 2 sounds (e.g., *b, b*) and if they are the same the child responds by saying "*Yes-Yes.*" If the sounds are different (e.g., *c, b*) then the child remains silent.
2. The teacher can mention words and have the child listen and react (e.g., *cat, cat; time, tin;* etc.).

variation: have the child listen for ending sounds, blends, and rhyming words.

Take a Vacation

purpose: to identify words orally that begin with a specific initial consonant sound
materials: an oral activity
procedure:
1. The teacher identifies a consonant that has been previously introduced to the class (e.g., *b*).

2. Each child in turn thinks of something to take on his vacation that begins with the identified consonant.

3. The first child could say, "I'm going on a vacation and I'm going to take a *b*all."

4. The next child repeats the sentence and adds his word.

5. For example, the second child could say, "I'm going on a vacation and I'm going to take my *b*unny."

6. The game continues until no one can think of any more *b* items. Then another consonant can be reviewed in the same manner.

Locate It

purpose: to identify initial consonants orally
materials: chalkboard and chalk
procedure:
1.   The teacher writes a word from the child's vocabulary on the chalk-board.

> **Example:**   pet

2.   The child locates and names objects in the room that begin like the "model."

> **Example:**   paper, Pat, paint, purple, etc.

Camera Game

purpose: to identify the missing sound orally
materials: chalkboard and chalk
procedure:
1.   The teacher writes several sounds on the board.

> **Example:**   *bl*   *a*   *b*   *z*   *t*   *qu*

2.   The children are told to "take a picture," then cover their eyes.
3.   The teacher quickly erases 1 sound.
4.   The children then are told to open their eyes.
5.   The child who can repeat the missing sound orally receives 1 point.
6.   The game continues until many sounds are reviewed.

Lightning Rod

purpose: to identify words orally that begin with a specific initial consonant sound
materials: chalkboard and chalk
procedure:
1.   The group is divided into 2 teams with a scorekeeper for each team.
2.   In 1 minute, the teams name as many words as they can that begin with a designated sound (e.g., *m*).
3.   The scorekeeper keeps track of the number of correct responses and writes the number on the chalkboard.
4.   The teacher can act as the referee.
5.   The team with the most correct responses is the winner.

Can It!

purpose: to recognize and identify initial consonant sounds orally
materials: cans, old magazines, workbook pictures and scissors
procedure:
1. Provide a series of cans with a letter and corresponding picture displayed on the front.

    Example:

2. The children are to cut out magazine and workbook pictures that correspond to the beginning sounds indicated on the cans.
3. When several pictures have been cut out, each child holds up one, says its beginning sound and then places it in the correct can.
4. The child continues this procedure until all his or her pictures are dispersed correctly.
5. When the child is finished, the teacher can check for correct responses.

Tag-O!

purpose: to identify beginning consonants orally
materials: oaktag, old workbook pictures, a decorated box and Magic Markers
procedure:
1. Each child receives an oaktag game board that contains different initial consonants.

    Example:

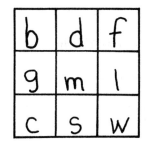

2. A series of pictured oaktag "tags" are placed in the decorated box.

    Examples for tags:

3. A caller (the teacher) pulls out a tag and names the picture (e.g., *kite*).
4. The child with the matching letter element orally identifies the beginning sound; if he is correct, he places the tag on the correct corresponding section of his card.
5. If the child is unable to identify the beginning consonant correctly, he loses his match.
6. The first child to fill in his card (straight across or up and down) yells out "Tag-O!" and is the winner.
7. The game can be stored in the decorated box.

Alike Words

purpose: to identify words orally that contain the same phonetic elements
materials: chalkboard, chalk and worksheet (See page 33.)
procedure:
1. The teacher writes and identifies a word from the child's vocabulary (e.g., *can*).
2. The teacher then pronounces a group of 3 words; 2 begin like the model and 1 does not (e.g., *cat, sat, can*).
3. The child listens and repeats only the 2 words that are *alike* and begin like the model.
4. The child then is given a follow-up worksheet on which he or she circles all the *alike words* in each row.

Key Words

purpose: to recognize and identify words beginning with familiar consonants
materials: chalkboard and chalk
procedure:
1. The teacher chooses at least 3 key words from a child's story that contains familiar beginning sounds and writes the key words on the board.

Worksheet

On   on   in   on

is   it   I   it

a   I   I   we

see   me   see   we

no   on   in   no

can   can   an   cot

Pet   let   me   Pet

ten   ben   get   get

bat   sat   me   sat

cat   cat   be   see

Example:

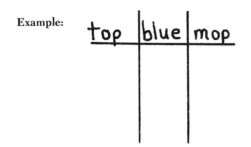

2. The child looks through the story and finds other words that begin the same as the key words.

3. When the child finds a related word, he or she orally says the word, then writes it on the board in the correct column.

Example:

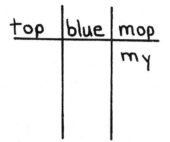

4. The child continues to find other related words and fills in the column.

Substitution

purpose: to identify orally and use consonants interchangeably
materials: chalkboard and chalk
procedure:
1. The teacher uses a word from the child's vocabulary and demonstrates that by substituting different initial consonants, new words can be formed.

Example: <u>t</u>ake = <u>m</u>ake; <u>m</u>ake = <u>b</u>ake.

2. The teacher writes known words on the board and the child reads the words.

Example: sat, can, wish, game.

3. The child orally identifies and adds a different initial consonant to each word ending to form as many new words as possible.

Example:	sat	can	wish	game
	mat	fan	fish	fame
	cat	ran	dish	same

2 motor response reading activities

Motor response reading activities further refine abilities initially encountered and developed in the previous chapter. This is not to say that the oral activities should be used prior to introducing motor skills; rather, the activities should be used in harmony.

Motor activities require the child to listen and do something; that is, after the student receives appropriate instructions, he or she responds through physical activity in the form of writing or some other action. The materials that follow are designed to develop fine motor coordination by utilizing the sense of touch, and large motor coordination by involving the student's total body. In effect, these activities integrate the body senses into the reading program to stimulate the student and provide for meaningful instruction.

Record Fun

purpose: to listen and record reactions
materials: record player, record (any record), drawing paper and crayons
procedure:
1. The teacher plays a record.
2. The children listen carefully.
3. The children then draw pictures or write words, thoughts or actions that come to mind.
4. The finished projects can be displayed.
5. A suggested caption for the display might be, "We *record* our thoughts."

Bumpity-Bump

purpose: to provide practice in forming letters through a tactile approach
materials: chalkboard, chalk and textured material (e.g., placemat,

plywood, corduroy, corrugated cardboard, sandpaper, and/or velvet)

procedure:

1. The teacher constructs large (i.e., child-size) letters from various materials.

   Example:

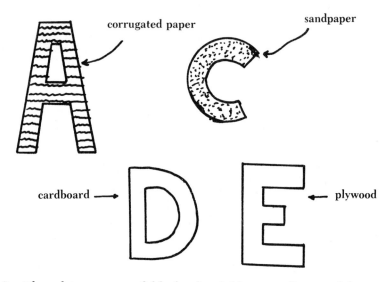

2. These letters are available for the children to roll over, slide across, lay on and, of course, feel and touch.

3. Then each child receives a piece of textured material.

4. The teacher writes a letter or word on the board.

5. The children watch carefully and then practice writing (finger writing) the letter or word onto their textured material.

6. This procedure is repeated until several letters and/or words have been reviewed.

Sandy Letters

purpose: to provide practice in forming letters through a tactile approach

materials: white glue, sand, oaktag paper, drawing paper, crayons and a decorated box

procedure:

1. The teacher makes a set of sand letters. (The letters are made by outlining the alphabet letters with glue on separate squares of oaktag, then sprinkling sand over the glue. The excess sand should be shaken off.)

Example:

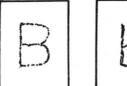

2. Each child chooses a letter to feel and trace with his or her finger. The letter card then is turned face down.
3. The child then reproduces that same letter on drawing paper with a crayon.
4. The crayon drawing is checked against the sand letter.
5. The sand cards can be stored in a decorated box.

variation: make sand cards displaying shapes, blends, sight words, etc.

What's Your Racket?

purpose: to provide practice in writing letters and words
materials: paper, pencil, chalk, chalkboard and worksheet (See page 40.)
procedure:
1. The teacher draws a tennis racket on the board with a tic-tac-toe square drawn on the face of the racket.

Example:

2. The teacher selects 2 letters, sounds or words to be reviewed (e.g., *f* and *v*).
3. Selecting a child from the class, the teacher and the child play tic-tac-toe on the tennis racket.

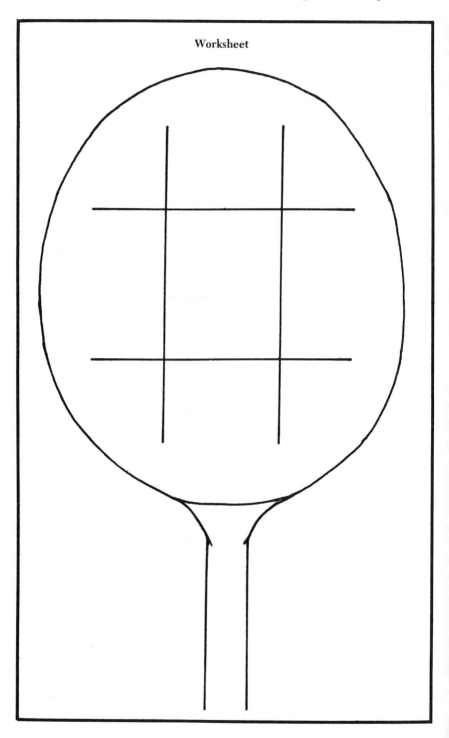

Worksheet

Example:

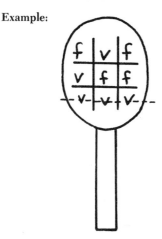

4. The teacher then provides the children with worksheets. The children should be paired so that they can play tic-tac-toe on the worksheets.

5. The teacher assigns 2 review letters (or sounds) to the class (e.g., *f* and *v*; *m* and *n*; etc.).

6. The children should take turns using the different letters.

variation: use 2 words that are to be reviewed.

Example:

Sounds on Parade

purpose: to identify letters and corresponding sounds
materials: letter cards, record player and record
procedure:
  1. The children form a circle and parade around to the tune of the music.

2. As one of the children passes the teacher he or she is given a letter card. (No one else sees the card except that one student.)
3. The teacher then stops the music.
4. The child with the letter card then imitates the sound of the letter on the card.
5. The other children try and guess what letter it is.
6. If there is an incorrect response, try again.
7. If the response is correct, the teacher collects the letter card and the parade continues.

Blind Fun

purpose: to identify letters and sounds through a tactile approach
materials: a decorated shoebox, alphabet letters (made out of wood, plastic, tile, cardboard or felt) and a blindfold
procedure:
1. The letters are placed in the decorated shoebox.
2. The child puts on the blindfold then reaches into the shoebox and pulls out a letter.
3. The child feels and touches the letter and attempts to identify the letter and its sound. The child also may repeat a word that begins with that sound (e.g., r, *rabbit*).
4. Then the child takes off the blindfold and checks to see if his or her response is correct.

Pudding Response

purpose: to provide practice in identifying sounds through a tactile approach
materials: pudding, clean surface (top of desk) and picture cards
procedure:
1. The teacher gives each child a scoop of pudding on his desk.
2. The teacher holds up a picture card and the child "pudding writes" on his desk the sound being reviewed (e.g., beginning, ending, blend, vowel, etc.).

Example:

3. Before going on to the next sound, the children lick their fingers clean and get ready for the next picture card.

4. For a very special treat, let the children make the letters with their tongues (tongue paint).

Puppet People

purpose: to provide practice in identifying beginning consonants
materials: oaktag, magazines, scissors, paste and crayons
procedure:
   1. Each child makes a person out of oaktag paper.

   Example:

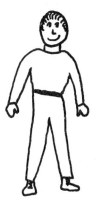

   2. Each child is assigned a sound to write on his or her puppet.

   Example:

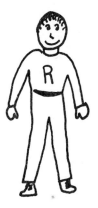

   3. The child then cuts out magazine pictures that contain the same corresponding sound and pastes the picture on his or her puppet. (Use both the front and back.)

   4. When the project is finished the "puppet people" are hung from the classroom ceiling.

Worksheet

man	fan	dog
top	can	mop
look	book	ball
house	boat	goat
see	bar	tree
cot	car	bar
name	game	bake
hill	him	fill
home	horn	corn

Take Away

purpose: to identify ending consonants
materials: picture cards, pocket chart and worksheet (See page 44.)
procedure:
   1.   The teacher places 3 picture cards in the pocket chart.

   Example:

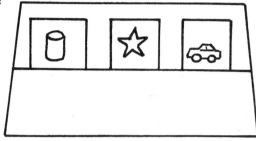

   2.   The teacher asks the child to "take away" the 1 that ends differently.
   3.   The child looks at the picture and finds the 1 that has a different ending from the rest (example, [image] can) and takes it out of the pocket chart.
   4.   The teacher proceeds with the activity by placing 3 or more cards in the pocket chart.
   5.   At the end of the activity, a follow-up worksheet is given to each child. The child is to take away (cross out) the word in each row that does not end like the rest.

Suitcase Game

purpose: to identify blends and their corresponding sounds
materials: chalkboard chalk, and worksheet (See page 46.)
procedure:
   1.   The class (or smaller group of students) is divided into 2 teams.
   2.   The teacher draws a suitcase on the board (1 for each team) and writes a blend on each suitcase.

   Example: Team #1   Team #2

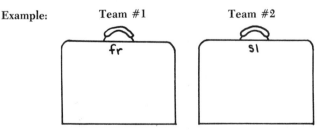

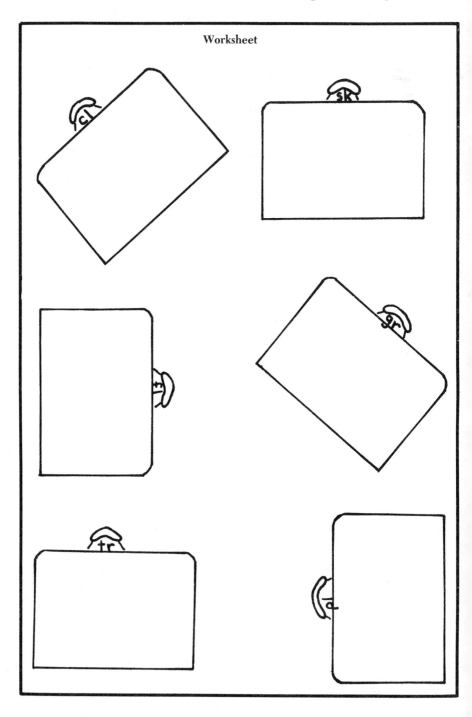

Worksheet

3. Each team writes sound-related words on their suitcase. The words may be obtained from the childrens' readers or from their word banks.

4. After approximately 2 minutes, the teacher calls out "Time up" and the team with the most words in their suitcase is the winner.

5. A follow-up worksheet then is given to each participating student. Each child is to fill his or her suitcase by writing familiar words from the basal reader.

variation: have the children cut out magazine words and/or pictures that contain the corresponding sounds.

Fish Pond

purpose: to provide practice in identifying sounds
materials: construction paper fish (See page 48 for fish pattern.)
procedure:
1. The fish have pictures (hand drawn or old workbook pictures) and word parts on them.

Example:

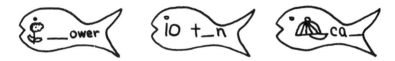

2. The fish are placed on a table (pond).

3. The child nets a fish (picks it up) and orally identifies the picture and the missing sound.

Make-a-Flower

purpose: to identify vowel sounds
materials: construction paper, scissors, paste, magazines and pencil
procedure:
1. The teacher gives each child a construction paper circle with a vowel sound written in the center.

Example:

Worksheet

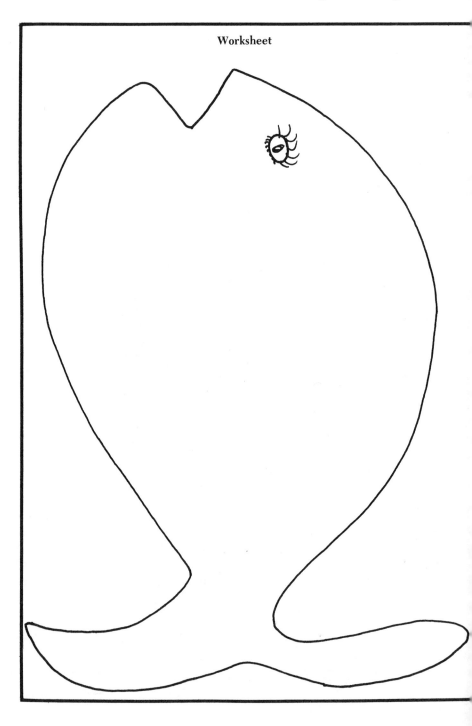

2. The children are to make petals for their flowers using construction paper.

3. Each petal must contain a different word and/or picture (cut from magazines) that relates to the sound in the flower center. The children add as many petals as they can.

   Example:

4. A stem and leaves can be added using left over construction paper.

Blow-Up!

purpose: to identify vowel sounds
materials: balloons and worksheet (See page 50.)
procedure:
1. Words with missing vowels have been previously written on the balloons by the teacher.

   Example:

2. Each child in a small group (4 or 5 members) is given a deflated balloon.

3. One child inflates his or her balloon and shows it to the group members.

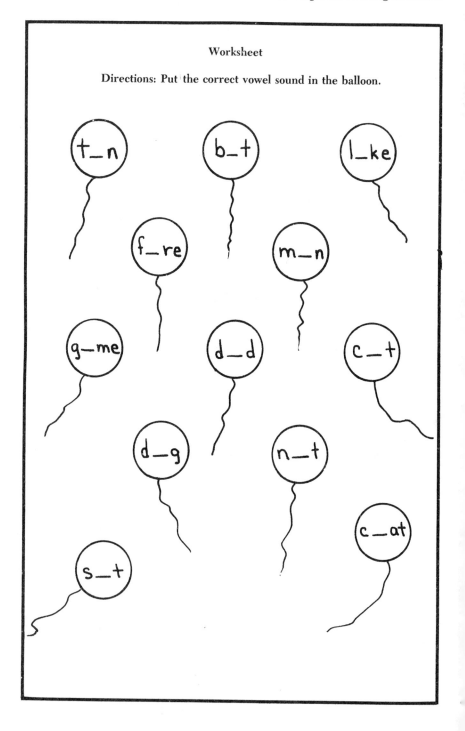

Worksheet

Directions: Put the correct vowel sound in the balloon.

4. The first child in the group to identify the word and vowel sound shouts it out and is the winner.

5. The winner gets to pop the balloon by either sitting or stepping on it.

6. The children will get a real *bang* out of this activity.

7. The children then fill in the missing letters on the follow-up worksheet.

Word-Bank Activity

purpose: to provide practice in identifying sounds

materials: chalkboard, chalk, student word banks and word cards, pencil and paper

procedure:

1. The teacher writes the sounds to be reviewed on the chalkboard.

    Example: bl   a   sh   or

2. The children, using their individual word banks, look through their words and make a list of words that contain the sounds the teacher is reviewing.

    Example: *bl*   *a*   *sh*   *or*
    blue   cake   she   horn

3 picture clues for reading reinforcement

The activities in this chapter provide the student with practical identification practice; thus, pictures are employed by the teacher as learning clues. Pictures help the child to identify objects, symbols, sounds, words, expressions, etc., and also help to unlock new words or to review previously learned concepts. Valuable reinforcement tools, picture clues are especially useful for beginning reading programs.

The materials that follow provide for matching words, expressions, objects, etc., with pictures in a wide variety of situations. Depending upon the child's education level and capacity, the activities may be teacher-implemented, or the student may solve the problems himself. In either event, numerous worksheets are supplied to serve as follow-up and reinforcement projects.

Picture Bingo

purpose: to provide practice in identifying like objects
materials: bingo boards with pictures, a series of individual matching pictures and worksheet (See page 54.)

Example:

 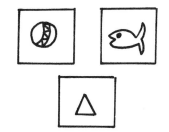

Make several picture boards (each different) with corresponding individual pictures for matching.

Worksheet
Directions: Match the like pictures.

procedure:

1. Each child receives a picture bingo board.
2. The first child draws a picture card from the pile and makes a match on his or her board, if possible.
3. If the drawn picture card doesn't match the child's board, another child in the group may claim the card if he or she has a match.
4. The game continues, each child drawing in turn, until someone has made "picture bingo" by filling in a card.

Weather Report

purpose: to identify weather words and symbols
materials: weather chart, weather words and worksheet (See page 56.)

Example:

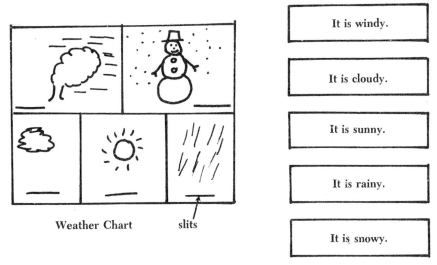

Weather Chart   slits

It is windy.

It is cloudy.

It is sunny.

It is rainy.

It is snowy.

procedure:

1. The teacher makes the weather report a daily procedure.
2. The group decides what kind of a day it is (or someone can be assigned to use the office phone to dial the local weather forecast number, listen to the report and report to the group).
3. The correct weather sentence then is matched to the weather symbol(s).
4. The class reads the report orally using the weather symbols to help unlock words.
5. A worksheet is given to each child in the group. The child is to cut out

Worksheet

Sunny

Windy

Sunny

Snowy

Cloudy

rainy

the weather word and paste it under the correct picture. The group weather chart can be used as a guide.

Fire Drill

purpose: to provide practice in relating and sequencing steps of a school rule

materials: chart paper and Magic Marker

procedure:

1. The teacher reviews the procedures for a fire drill. As the procedure is reviewed, the teacher describes the sequential steps of the event.

2. The children listen carefully.

3. The children then act out and go through the actual steps involved in a school fire drill.

4. The children then gather in front of the chart paper.

5. The children dictate each important fire drill step to the teacher.

6. The teacher *records* and *illustrates* the procedures on the chart paper.

> **Example:** *Fire Drill*
> 1. Put your work away.
> 2. Line up quietly.
> 3. Walk quietly outside.
> 4. Someone should turn off the lights and close the classroom door.
> 5. Wait outside quietly for the "o.k." bell.
> 6. Come back inside quietly.
> 7. Continue to do your work.

7. The children attempt to read the chart using the picture clues to help unlock words.

Picture and Spoken Word Game

purpose: to associate pictures with spoken words

materials: picture cards

procedure:

1. The teacher displays several picture cards on the chalkboard.

2. The teacher says a word (e.g., *boy*) then says a sentence in which he or she emphasizes the key word (e.g., "The *boy* is little.").

3. The teacher asks a child to find the picture card that relates to the key word.

Worksheet
Directions: Match the picture and the beginning sound.

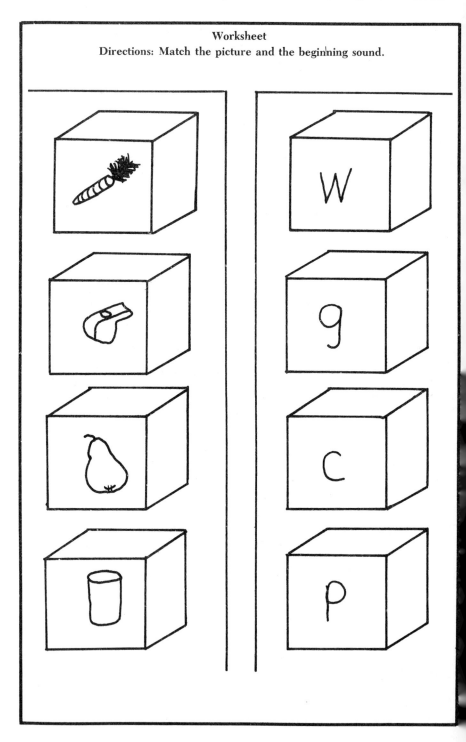

variation: this activity may be developed further by writing sentences on strips of paper with certain words underlined. The child is then required to find the picture that matches the underlined word.

Roll-Em

purpose: to match pictures and beginning consonant sounds

materials: several cubical blocks, several small rubber balls, several sponge squares, Magic Markers (permanent ink) and worksheet (See page 58.)

procedure:

1. The teacher has a set of blocks, a set of sponge squares and a set of balls with hand-drawn pictures and consonant sounds written on them.

   Example:

   Blocks   Balls   Sponges

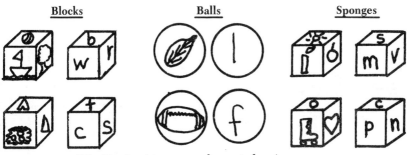

   (Workbook pictures may be pasted on.)

2. The child rolls the blocks and finds as many pairs as possible by matching a picture block with its beginning sound.

3. The child follows the same procedure with the sponge squares.

4. The balls are sorted and matched correctly. Also, the child may bounce 1 ball (e.g., the p ball) and repeat as many p words as he or she can, 1 word for each bounce.

Dog and Bone

purpose: to match pictures and consonant sounds

materials: construction paper dogs, construction paper bones (with pictures drawn or pasted on them), paper clips and envelope

procedure:

1. The dogs and their bones are displayed on a large chart or bulletin board.

2. Each dog has a sound printed on it.

Example:

paper
clips

pictures
bones

3. The child takes a pictured bone out of the envelope and matches it to the corresponding dog. (Paper clips are used to hold the bones on the dog.)

4. This is a good activity to get the children to "bone up" on their sounds.

Card Game

purpose: to identify and match pictures and consonant sounds
materials: picture cards and letter cards
procedure:
1. The teacher places 6 letter cards face up on the table.

Example:

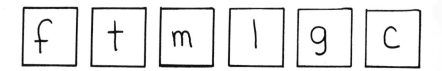

2. The picture cards then are placed face down in a pile.
3. The children take turns drawing 1 picture card at a time from the pile.
4. If the drawn picture card matches one of the consonant sounds (beginning or ending) on the table, the child places it under the letter card.
5. If the drawn card does not match any of the letter cards, it is set aside.
6. The game continues until all the correct picture cards are matched with the correct letter cards.

Example:

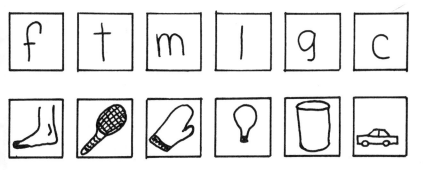

7. The teacher can change the letter cards, and the game begins again.

Alphabet Letters

purpose: to identify beginning sounds
materials: large pictures (from magazines, newspapers, calendars, workbooks, charts, etc.), alphabet macaroni and paste
procedure:
1. Each child chooses a picture and then receives a handful of macaroni.

2. The directions are to look carefully at the picture and label everything in the picture with its beginning sound using the alphabet macaroni.

Example:

3. When the children have completed this activity, the pictures can be displayed in the room. The caption could be "Picture This."

Can You Cross the Bridge?

purpose: to identify the missing phonetic sound
materials: oaktag game board, Magic Markers, picture cards (including part of the word) and markers

Example:

Game Board

Picture Cards

procedure:
1. The picture cards are placed face down in the upper left corner of the game board.
2. The first player takes the top card and identifies the missing sound (using the picture as a clue).
3. The child self-checks his or her response by checking the back of the picture card.
4. If the child's answer is correct, he moves his marker 1 space on the bridge.
5. If the child's response is incorrect he loses his turn.
6. The first child to cross over the bridge is the winner.

Slit-a-Word

purpose: to match pictures and sounds
materials: pictures, notebook, sound cards and envelope (to store the sound cards)
procedure:
1. The teacher compiles a notebook of pictures with slits on the opposite pages. The teacher also makes corresponding sound cards.

Example:

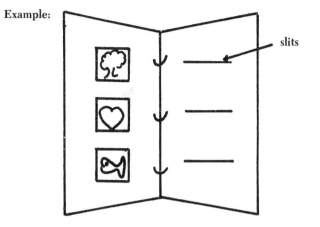

2. The child opens the notebook and attempts to do the first page.

3. The child looks through the sound cards and matches a sound with the first picture, etc. The child can choose to match the beginning, middle or ending sound, or as the teacher directs.

Example:

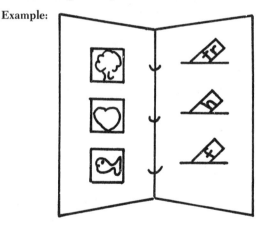

4. The child continues to work through the notebook until all pages are complete.

5. When all the pages are completed, the child takes the notebook to the teacher for on-the-spot checking.

Bag-It

purpose: to be able to associate words and pictures
materials: small lunch bags, workbook pictures and Magic Marker

procedure:
1. The teacher makes individual bags for each child. Each bag consists of a cut-out picture pasted on the front and is labeled.

   Example:

2. The child takes his or her bag home and fills it with related words and/or pictures cut from magazines.

   Example:

 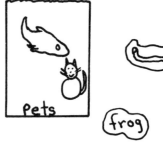

3. The next day, the children share their bags with each other.

Happy Holiday

purpose: to match words and pictures
materials: holiday picture cards, holiday word cards, a pocket chart and a worksheet (See page 65.)
procedure:
1. The teacher displays holiday pictures and holiday word cards in a pocket chart.

   Example:

Worksheet

Directions: Cut and paste the correct holiday words under the correct picture.

2. The child looks carefully at the pictures and word cards and decides which ones match.

3. The child then pairs the correct cards together by displaying them in the pocket chart.

    Example:

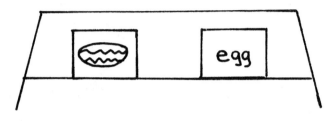

4. The activity can continue with the teacher placing more picture and word cards in the chart.

Be Mobile

purpose: to match pictures and words
materials: coat hangers, masking tape, pictures, word cards with paper clips attached, thread and loose spring
procedure:
1. The teacher makes a mobile by crossing 2 coat hangers and securing them with masking tape.

2. Pictures are hung from the mobile using thread. The coat hanger mobile is hung from a loose string attached to the ceiling, bulletin board or over the chalk board.

3. When the mobile is in use, the teacher pulls it down so that it is at the child's eye level. Either the teacher or another child may hold the mobile at the correct height.

4. The child is to look through the word cards and match the correct word with the correct picture.

5. The word is attached to the picture card with the paper clip.

6. When the mobile has been labeled completely, the holder releases it.

7. The mobile makes a nice classroom display.

Bird Bingo

purpose: to associate spoken words with pictures
materials: "bird" bingo cards and markers

Example:

B	I	R	D	S
Sparrow	jay	robin	pigeon	duck
parrot	canary	crow	turkey	goose

Make several different cards including bird names and their pictures.

procedure:
1. The teacher calls out the names of birds.
2. The child covers the picture with a marker if it appears on his or her card.
3. The first child to fill in a row across is the winner.
4. If the children lack experience in identifying birds, a large chart displaying birds and their names will help.

variation: make cards for flowers, animals, foods, etc.

What Am I?

purpose: to associate pictures and riddles
materials: picture cards, riddles and pocket chart
procedure:
1. The teacher displays pictures and a riddle in the pocket chart.

Example:

I have hands but cannot feel.

2. The child silently reads the riddle carefully.

3. The child selects the correct picture.

    Example:

4. The child then reads the riddle and answer aloud.
5. The teacher displays other pictures and riddles.
6. Other riddles could be as follows:

> I have eyes but cannot see. (potato)
> I have ears but cannot hear. (corn)
> I have legs but cannot walk. (table, chair)
> I have a tongue but cannot talk. (shoe)
> I have teeth but cannot chew. (comb, saw)

Supply the Missing Word

purpose: to identify the missing word
materials: picture cards, sentence strips (with a word missing) and pocket chart
procedure:

1. The teacher displays a sentence strip and 2 pictures in the pocket chart.

    Example:

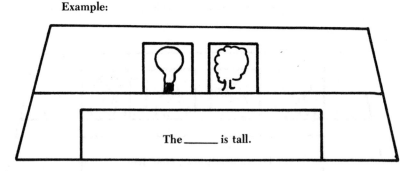

2. The child reads carefully and decides which picture (and word) will supply the missing word.

3. The child chooses 1 and rereads the sentence using his or her choice.

4. The teacher then displays another sentence strip and 2 more pictures.

Phrase Race!

purpose: to associate phrases and pictures
materials: picture cards, phrase cards and pocket chart
procedure:
1. The teacher displays a picture and 3 phrase cards in a pocket chart.

   Example:

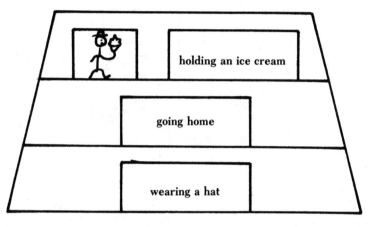

2. Two children play at a time, and each reads the phrases silently.

3. At a signal from the teacher, the children race to the chart.

4. The first child to arrive at the chart must remove the phrase card that *does not* associate with the picture.

5. If the first child is incorrect, the phrase card is replaced in the pocket chart and the other child gets to select.

6. The child that is correct gets a point. If neither child is correct, neither receives a point.

variation: the phrase race game also can be played with 2 teams.

Picture Clues

purpose: to match pictures and related sentences
materials: picture cards, sentence strips, pocket chart and worksheet (See page 70.)

Worksheet

I am a bird.
I live in a tree.

I am a rabbit.

I see 2 flowers.

I see 3 flowers.

The flowers are pretty.

This is a tree.

There are apples on the tree.

I see 5 apples.

I am a snowman.

I have 3 eyes.

I melt in the sun.

We are ghosts.

We are bears.

We like to scare people.

I see 3 balloons.

I see 4 balloons.

I see 5 balloons.

The sun is hot.

It is a sailboat.

It is raining.

One fish is wearing a coat.

There are 3 fish.

The fish can swim.

procedure:
1. The teacher displays 1 picture at a time and a series of sentence strips. (Use a pocket chart.)

      Example:

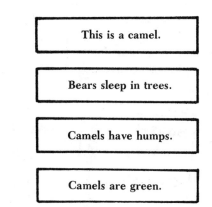

2. The child selects from a group of sentences those strips that could be used to describe the picture.
3. The child places the correct sentence strips next to or under the picture card.
4. A follow-up worksheet is then given to each child. The child is to draw a line from the picture to the correct sentences in each block.

      Example:

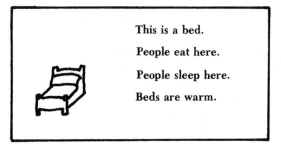

Be a Booky

purpose: to associate sentences with book jackets
materials: sentence strips, yarn, paper clips and book jackets (obtained from the school media center)
procedure:
1. The teacher displays the sentence strips and book jackets on a large

chart or bulletin board. A piece of yarn is attached to each sentence strip.

Example:

2. The child is to read the sentence and match the yarn to the correct book jacket. The yarn is attached to the book with a paper clip.

3. When the activity is completed, the teacher checks the child's choices and goes over the activity orally with the child.

What's the Conversation?

purpose: to associate conversation with picture characters
materials: drawing paper, crayons and Basal Readers
procedure:

1. The children are to use their readers and choose a favorite story character (or characters).

2. The children draw a picture of the character and write what the character might be saying.

Example:

3. Also, the children can draw a picture of more than 1 character and write captions.

> **Example:**

4. The children may continue the same procedure with other story characters, or they can involve many characters in a common conversation.

Finger Magic

purpose: to recognize meaningful and meaningless sentences
materials: Magic Markers (washable ink)
procedure:
1. The children draw a happy face on 1 finger and a sad face on another finger.

> **Example:**

2. The teacher reads a sentence that directs an activity.
3. If the sentence makes sense, the children acknowledge by wiggling the happy-faced finger.
4. If the sentence is meaningless, then the children wiggle the sad-faced finger.

> **Example:**   Smack your lips.

Hear the wall.

Jump up and down.

variation: respond to the meaningless sentences by doing nothing and if the sentence is meaningful, the children can act it out.

4   unlocking meanings with context clues

In this chapter "context clue" activities are recommended to assist the child in interpreting new or difficult words from surrounding words and phrases, discriminating between relevant and irrelevant information, and providing practice in meaningful sentence construction.

The materials included in this chapter assist the student in "unlocking" the meanings of words or phonetic elements by using the "context" of the sentence or story. In addition, the student is given practice in eliminating words and/or sentences that do not belong in the context presented. Finally, follow-up worksheets are provided for review and additional practice.

Does It Make Sense?

purpose: to identify meaningful sentences
materials: sentence strips and worksheet (See page 76.)
procedure:

1. The teacher displays 1 sentence at a time on the chalk ledge.

    Example: | A cat says bow-wow. | | Tom can jump. |

2. The children read the sentence silently and decide if it makes sense.

3. If the sentence makes sense, they respond by shaking their heads up and down. The "yes" response can be varied each time (e.g., wriggle your nose, pat your head, smack your lips, give a one-hand clap, stamp your feet, etc.).

4. If the sentence does not make sense, the children remain silent.

5. When the activity is completed, the group is given a follow-up worksheet on which they are to read each sentence and circle "yes" if it makes sense and "no" if it does not.

Worksheet

Directions: Circle "yes" if the sentence makes sense and "no" if it does not.

A dog can bark.	Yes	No
A clown is funny.	Yes	No
Jill can fly.	Yes	No
A kitten is little.	Yes	No
A baby is big.	Yes	No
Flowers grow in dirt.	Yes	No
Tom can run fast.	Yes	No
We can eat wood.	Yes	No
A boat sails on land.	Yes	No

Hodgepodge

purpose: to identify meaningful sentences

materials: sentence strips (meaningful sentences and the same sentences with words mixed up)

Example:

The tree is green.	green tree The is.
The apple is sweet.	sweet is apple The.

procedure:

1. The group is divided in 2.
2. One half of the children are given the meaningful sentences and the other half the hodgepodge sentences.
3. The children read their sentence strips.
4. The child with the hodgepodge sentence must match him or herself with the student holding the meaningful sentence.
5. The first individual to find his or her partner yells "Hodgepodge" and is the winner.
6. The teacher checks to make sure the match is correct. If the match is correct, the teacher collects the cards, redistributes them and the game continues. If the match is incorrect, the game continues until a correct match is made.

Scrambled!

purpose: to make meaningful sentences
materials: an oral activity and a worksheet (See below.)
procedure:

1. The teacher reads a scrambled sentence. (Start with the simple and work toward the complex.)

> **Example:** boy I a see.
> The fat is pig pink.

2. The children listen and unscramble the words orally, and then repeat the meaningful sentence.

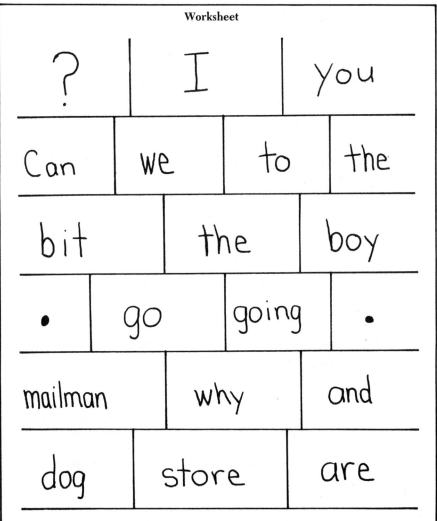

Worksheet

?	I	you
Can	we	to	the
bit	the	boy
.	go	going	.
mailman	why	and
dog	store	are

3. The teacher repeats the activity.

4. Each child is then given a follow-up worksheet. The children are to cut out the words and build as many sentences as they can. They may build the sentences on their desk or paste them on other sheets of paper.

Leave It Out

purpose: to identify the sentence that does not fit the story
materials: chart paper, Magic Markers and a strip of oaktag
procedure:
1. The teacher writes a paragraph on chart paper.

    Example:

> Mother made a pie.
>
> Sue made some cookies.
>
> The sun is hot.
>
> Mother put a cherry on top of the pie.
>
> Sue put frosting on top of the cookies.

2. The child reads the paragraph and identifies the sentence that does not belong.

3. The child takes the oaktag strip and covers the sentence that does not belong.

4. The teacher continues the activity with other paragraphs.

Six Words

purpose: to supply the missing word using context clues
materials: an oral activity
procedure:
1. The teacher reads a story, leaving out 6 words.

2. The children listen carefully and respond by trying to supply the correct word. (Any word is acceptable as long as it fits the context of the story.)

    Example: There once was a little mouse named_____ . The mouse loved to eat cheese and_____ . He would take cheese from the neighborhood_____ . He would_____the food in his little mouse_____. During the winter months he had _____ to eat.

Mail Me

purpose: to identify the missing word using context clues
materials: oaktag, Magic Markers, words cards and a decorated box (for storing word cards)
procedure:
1. Make several mailboxes out of oaktag. At the bottom of each mailbox write a sentence with a word omitted.

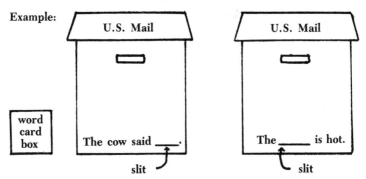

2. The child chooses the correct word card from the decorated box and matches it with the correct mailbox.
3. The child *mails* his or her word card by inserting it into the slit in the sentence and then rereads the sentence to make sure it makes sense.

variation: this activity may include *mailing* phrases, punctuation marks, etc.

Be a Detective

purpose: to identify key words using context clues
materials: sentence strips (with 1 word omitted) and worksheet (See page 80.)
procedure:
1. The teacher places a sentence strip on the chalkboard.

Example: The dog jumped over the _____ .

2. The child reads the sentence and responds by supplying a word that gives the sentence meaning.
3. The teacher continues the activity by displaying other sentence strips.
4. A follow-up worksheet then is given to each child. The child is to be a

detective and choose the correct word from the clue box and write it in the correct space.

Worksheet

Be a Detective

1. The _____ jumped over the moon.

2. The man painted the _____ .

3. The dog _____ down the street.

4. The boy can run _____ .

5. _____ said, "I am hungry."

6. The tree has many _____ .

7. There are six _____ on the cake.

8. The cat had _____ .

9. Animals live on the _____ .

Clue Box

fast	candles
Tom	kittens
leaves	farm
house	ran
cow	

Meaningful Sentences

purpose: to provide practice in completing meaningful sentences
materials: sentence strips, finger paint and finger paint paper
procedure:
1. The teacher displays incomplete sentences on the chalk ledge.

Example:
> The cat felt _____ .
> Then the cat saw a _____ and a _____ .
> Clues: boy, sad, girl

2. The children are given finger paint and paper.
3. The children finger paint the correct choice of words on the paper.

Example:

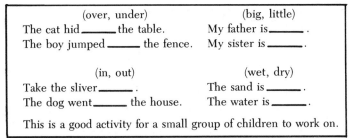

4. The children then hold up their papers for all to see and for checking.
5. The children scribble out their responses and get ready for the next set of sentences.

Contrasting Words

purpose: to complete sentences with contrasting words
materials: mural paper and Magic Marker
procedure:
1. The teacher prepares incomplete sentences on mural paper.
   Example:

(over, under)	(big, little)
The cat hid _____ the table.	My father is _____ .
The boy jumped _____ the fence.	My sister is _____ .
(in, out)	(wet, dry)
Take the sliver _____ .	The sand is _____ .
The dog went _____ the house.	The water is _____ .

   This is a good activity for a small group of children to work on.

2. The group is presented the mural. They are to complete the sentences by writing in the correct contrasting word.
3. When completed, the mural is checked by the teacher and displayed in the room.
4. The mural caption might be "Learning Can Be Contrasting."

Puzzled?

purpose: to associate sentences with puzzles
materials: simple puzzles, a box containing related sentence strips and manila folders (to hold puzzle parts)
procedure:
1. The child assembles a puzzle that he or she has selected from a manila folder.
2. The child then selects a sentence strip that corresponds with the puzzle he or she has assembled.

3. The puzzle and sentence strip can be coded for self-checking.

4. This can prove to be a puzzling, but fun activity for the children.

Draw It

purpose: to draw pictures of key words in context
materials: sentence strips, drawing paper and crayons
procedure:

1. The teacher displays several sentence strips on the chalkboard. Key words are underlined.

> **Example:** The <u>dog</u> is little.
>
> The <u>house</u> is red.
>
> I read a funny <u>book.</u>

2. The children or the teacher reads the sentences.

3. Then the children are given paper and crayons.

4. The children draw pictures to represent the underlined words.

5. The children's drawings and the related sentence strips can be displayed in the classroom.

Homographs

purpose: using context clues to determine word meaning
materials: homograph picture cards and sentence strips

> **Example:**   **Homograph Cards**

procedure:
1. The teacher holds up a sentence strip with a word underlined.
2. The teacher also displays the corresponding homograph card.
3. The child indicates by number the picture that corresponds with the context of the sentence.

    Example: | The bark is brown. | (Answer: Number 1)

4. Several other examples of homographs are as follows:

    Water well, and I feel well.
    Palm (tree) and palm (hand)
    File (nail) and file (cabinet).
    Nail (finger) and nail (as with hammer).
    Pen (writing) and pen (animal).
    Top (table) and top (toy).

Related Words

purpose: to match related words
materials: oaktag, colored pipe cleaners and Magic Markers
procedure:
1. The teacher prepares several oaktag squares with related words written on them.

    Example:

Tom sails	red color	shoes head
rose boy	sun Sue	hat feet
boat pet	apple fruit	pie door
cat stem	girl hot	house desert

2. A hole is punched next to each word, and a different colored pipe cleaner is inserted in the hole next to each word on the left.

    Example:

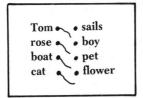

Tom • sails
rose • boy
boat • pet
cat • flower

Use different-colored pipe cleaners.

3. The child is given a card and matches the related words.

Example:

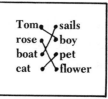

4. The child then turns the card over for self-checking.

Example:

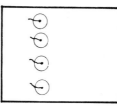

**Color code answers
to different-colored
pipe cleaners.**

5. If the card is correct, the colored pipe cleaners will correspond to the colored circles on the back.

Sentence Game

purpose: to make meaningful sentences
materials: word cards (basic words, such as from the Dolch list)
procedure:
1. The word cards are placed face down on the table.
2. Each child (a game for 2-4 children) takes a word card from the top of the pile.
3. Each child continues to draw a card in turn until he or she can make a meaningful sentence.
4. The first child to make a sentence is the winner.
5. Then the cards are reshuffled and the game continues.

Eggs in a Basket

purpose: to make meaningful sentences
materials: oaktag eggs (containing parts of sentences), an oaktag basket, flannel, glue, flannel board and worksheet (See page 85.)
procedure:
1. A piece of flannel is glued on the back of the eggs and the basket.

Worksheet

Directions: Cut out the 2 phrases that make a meaningful
sentence and paste them on the line next to a number.

_____

1. _____

2. _____

3. _____

4. _____

The boy   The tree   ran fast

The house   is blue

Said meow

has leaves   The cat

2. The teacher displays the eggs and the basket on the flannel board.

   Example:

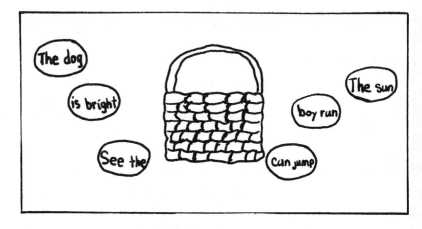

3. The children are to select 2 eggs to make a meaningful sentence and place them in the basket.
4. The activity continues until all eggs have been used.
5. The teacher then places other eggs on the flannel board and the activity continues.

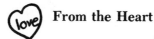 From the Heart

purpose: to make a meaningful sentence
materials: candy hearts
procedure:

1. This is a good activity for February.
2. The teacher gives each child approximately 15 or 20 candy hearts.
3. Each child tries to arrange his or her hearts and makes as many meaningful sentences as possible.
4. The child can try to create an original story.
5. Two children can work together and share hearts to build an interesting story.
6. After the sentences have been checked by the teacher, the children can eat the hearts.
7. The children enjoy working and getting "to the heart" of this activity.

Make a Sentence

purpose: to make meaningful sentences
materials: oaktag game board and phrase cards (an equal number of individual oaktag squares containing the beginning, middle and ending parts of sentences)

Example: Game Board

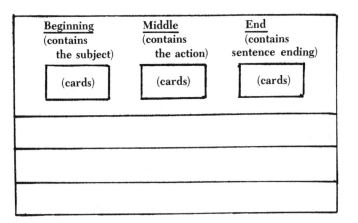

Phrase Cards

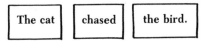

procedure:

1. The beginning, middle and ending phrase cards are arranged in individual piles on the game board.
2. The child sorts through each of the piles and, selecting 1 card from each pile, makes as many meaningful sentences as possible.
3. The completed sentences should be arranged in a row on the oaktag game board.
4. The child may work independently or with a partner or team.

Happy Endings

purpose: to identify sentence endings
materials: sentence strips (sentence without an ending), magazines, scissors, paste and worksheet (See page 88.)

procedure:
1.   The teacher shows the children a sentence strip.

>   **Example:** | The man ate _____ . |

2.   The children orally supply a meaningful ending.
3.   At the completion of the activity, the children are given a worksheet and a magazine. The children are to cut out and paste word endings on the worksheet to complete the sentences.

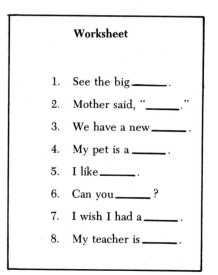

Worksheet

1.   See the big _____ .
2.   Mother said, "_____ ."
3.   We have a new _____ .
4.   My pet is a _____ .
5.   I like _____ .
6.   Can you _____ ?
7.   I wish I had a _____ .
8.   My teacher is _____ .

Under the Big Top

purpose: to identify the missing letters
materials: sentence strips, oaktag circus animals, worksheet (See page 89.)
procedure:
1.   The teacher displays several circus animals on a bulletin board with a sentence strip under each. In each sentence there are letters missing.
2.   The children are to supply the missing letters orally.
3.   The children then are given a follow-up worksheet on which they are to write in the missing letters in the spaces provided.

Example:

| The bea__ has a all on his hea__. | The __onkey is eatin__ a banana. | The lio__ said roa__. |

Worksheet

1. The sky is ⊵ lue.

2. I see something gree △.

3. My toy is a to ⧦.

4. The ⊴ ⅃ ip is big.

5. Fi ⊵ ⅃ can swim.

6. Did you ever see a c ▲ t?

7. The clow △ is ⌠ unny.

8. The ⌐ ouse i ⊃ gray.

9. The ⊃ now is cold.

5   strengthening recall abilities

Recall is the ability to identify and remember previously exposed letters, phonetic elements, words and concepts. Thus, recall activities are employed to repeat, review and reinforce learned material and to employ such material correctly.

The materials in this chapter generally require oral responses by the student. Furthermore, several activities require the child to follow certain directions. Since repetition is essential to effective reading, follow-up worksheets have been provided to assist in strengthening recall skills further.

Fruit Basket

purpose: to be able to recall visual elements

materials: pictures of fruit (mounted on individual pieces of oaktag), a basket and tape

procedure:

1. A child selects 5 fruit cards from the basket while the other players close their eyes.

2. The child places a small piece of tape on the back of 1 of the cards and hides that card.

3. The remaining 4 cards are turned face down on the table.

4. On signal, the players open their eyes and the hidden card is flashed before them.

5. The players again close their eyes. Thereafter, all 5 fruit cards are placed face up.

6. The players must pick out the fruit that was flashed.

7. The self-checking tape is on the back of the correct response.

Silhouette Fun

purpose: to be able to recall visual elements

materials: individual oaktag squares containing silhouette pictures (Make a
duplicate set.)

Example:

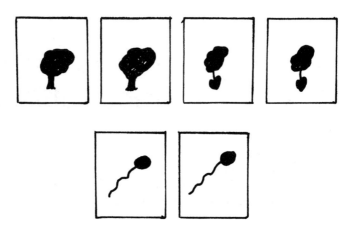

procedure:
1. The teacher places 3 or 4 silhouette cards on the chalk ledge. The
   cards are turned so the children cannot see the silhouettes.

2. From the duplicate set the teacher flashes 1 card for all to see. The
   flashed card should be the same as the one on the chalk ledge.

3. Then the teacher turns the chalk ledge cards around, and the children
   tell which one matches the flashed silhouette card.

Word Association

purpose: to be able to recall and associate word meanings
materials: a variety of picture cards
procedure:
1. The children are divided into 2 teams.

2. The teacher is the referee and shows a picture card (e.g., a candy
   cane) to the children, but says nothing.

3. The teacher points to the first child of 1 team, who mentions as many
   words as possible associated with candy cane (e.g., eat, sweet, etc.).

4. The referee counts 1 point for each correctly associated word.

5. The game continues with the teacher showing another picture card
   and pointing to the first person on the opposing team, etc.

6. When each child on each team has had a turn, the score is totaled.

Animals on the Farm

purpose: to be able to recall auditory elements
materials: an oral activity
procedure:
1. The teacher designates 1 child in the group as the "leader."
2. The leader begins the game by saying, "I'm thinking of a farm animal that I will describe to you. You must try to guess my animal. If anyone guesses incorrectly, he or she is out."
3. The leader then describes his animal (e.g., "My animal hatches from an egg. It has 2 legs.").
4. Some additional information might be added: "It lives on land and has feathers."
5. The child who correctly guesses *chicken* becomes the leader and has a turn to describe a farm animal.

variation: as a pre-activity, the children could be taken on a field trip to a farm.

Riddles

purpose: to recall rhyming words
materials: chart paper and Magic Marker
procedure:
1. The teacher writes and displays several riddles on chart paper.
2. The children take turns supplying the missing rhyming word or words as the teacher reads the riddles.
3. This is a fun activity to reinforce the rhyming concept, and any answer can be acceptable.
4. Let the children laugh and enjoy this activity.

> **Example:**   I am bright.
>
> I shine at night.
>
> I am _____ .

5. The children might answer by saying, "a light"; "a fat knight"; "a real sight"; "a yellow kite"; etc.

A-Shopping We Will Go

purpose: to recall the same beginning phonetic elements

materials: sentence strips and Magic Marker
procedure:
1. The teacher mentions to the group that they are all going shopping to the toy store.
2. Each child must tell what he or she will purchase, and the toy purchased must have the same phonetic element as his or her first name.
3. Each child's response is recorded on an individual sentence strip by the teacher.

> **Example:**   Bob will buy a ball.
>
> Jane will buy some jacks.
>
> Chuck will buy some chalk.

4. The sentence strips may be read orally by the children and displayed in the classroom.

Name-Game

purpose: to recall ending phonetic sounds
materials: a decorated box and oaktag paper
procedure:
1. The childrens' first names are written on individual pieces of oaktag.
2. The names are placed in the decorated box.
3. A child chooses a name from the box (e.g., *Sam*).
4. That child must say the person's name and give another word that begins with the ending sound of the name.

> **Example:**   Sam—Mouse

5. Each child in the group has a turn at drawing a name.

variation: use the drawn name and the response word in a sentence.

> **Example:**   Sam is as quiet as a mouse.

Grid and Bear It

purpose: to recall and identify ending sounds
materials: several lettered "Bear Grids" and markers
procedure:
1. Each child receives a different grid.
2. The teacher says a word (e.g., *Men*).
3. The children listen for the ending sound and if they have it on their grids, they place a marker on that letter (e.g., *n*).

4. The first child to get 3 in a row (down or across) is the winner or the "Big Bear."

Example:

Which Hand?

purpose: to identify objects and recall consonant sounds
materials: small objects
procedure:
1. The teacher places an object in each hand then closes her hands and puts them behind her back.
2. The first child chooses a hand.
3. That hand and the enclosed object are revealed.
4. The child must identify the object and recall a word or words that begin (or end) like the object in the teacher's hand.
5. Each child in the group gets a turn to choose a hand and identify the object.

Picture Dictionary

purpose: to recall consonant sounds
materials: manila drawing paper, stapler and crayons
procedure:
1. Each child makes a booklet by stapling several manila pages together.
2. The teacher writes a few words on the board that begin with the letter to be recalled.

      Example: Let

                   Look

                   Like

3. The child makes his or her first page in the dictionary by labeling the page with an "L," thinks of other things that begin with that sound, and then draws and labels pictures of things that contain the "L" sound.

4. The teacher proceeds to write sounds to be recalled, and the children continue to fill in the pages in their picture dictionaries.

5. The completed booklet is a nice reference and helps the children in the review of consonant sounds.

Spin Off

purpose: to recall beginning sounds
materials: circular pieces of oaktag, a numbered spinner, Magic Markers and brass fasteners
procedure:
1. The teacher makes several circular picture wheels.

   Example:

Each section is numbered to correspond with a spinner.

   Example:

2. Each child receives a different picture wheel.

3. The first child spins the spinner and then locates that number and picture on his or her picture wheel.

4. The child must identify that picture and give a word that begins with the same phonetic sound.

variation: the teacher asks the child to draw pictures that begin like the sounds on his or her picture wheel.

Let's Race

purpose: to recall and identify blends
materials: individual oaktag squares, Magic Markers, old magazines, scissors and glue
procedure:
  1.   The teacher writes a word on each oaktag square. Each word contains a blend that is to be reviewed.

Example: [Blue   ]

  2.   Each child in the group receives 1 word card, a magazine, scissors and glue.
  3.   Each child is to go through a magazine and find words and/or pictures that begin with the blend written on his or her word card. The pictures and/or words are pasted on the word card. (Use both front and back.)
  4.   A time limit should be set for this activity, and at the end of the race the child with the most correct pictures and/or words on his or her card is the winner.

Wow!

purpose: to recall auditory and visual ending elements
materials: oaktag, Magic Marker and worksheet (See page 98.)
procedure:
  1.   The teacher makes several different "Wow" cards. Each card has 9 sections and is headed by a key word and picture.

Example:

  2.   Also, several related word tags are made to match the ending sounds on the "Wow" cards.

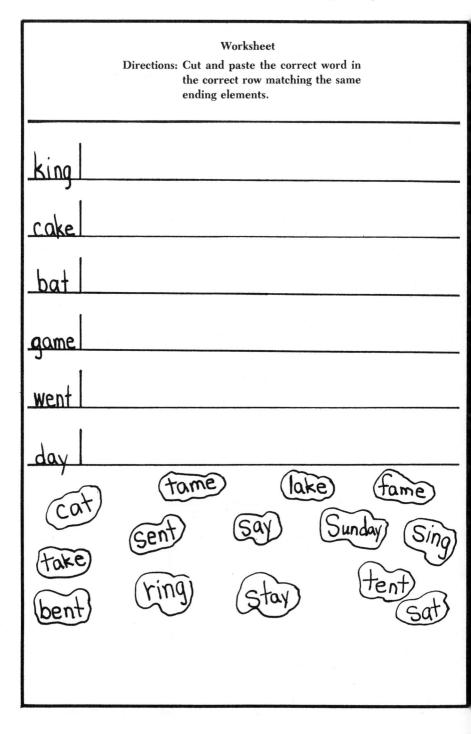

Worksheet

Directions: Cut and paste the correct word in
the correct row matching the same
ending elements.

king

cake

bat

game

went

day

cat · tame · lake · fame · sent · say · Sunday · Sing · take · ring · stay · tent · bent · sat

Example:

3. Each child receives a "Wow" card and is told to listen and match the ending element.

4. The word tags are placed in a pile, and the teacher draws 1 tag and holds it up.

5. The child that can use the tag to make a match on his or her "Wow" card says the word and places the tag in the correct section of the card.

6. The game continues until someone has filled in a complete card. That child yells out "Wow" and is the winner.

Make-a-Word

purpose: to recall phonetic elements and be able to form words
materials: oaktag, Magic Markers and markers
procedure:
1. The oaktag is cut into the size of playing cards. On the cards write consonant sounds, matrix (families), vowels, blends, digraphs and common double consonants. Some blank cards should be in the pack. The blanks stand for whatever symbols the child might need.

2. Each child is given 3 cards.

3. The players are to arrange their cards to make a word, and if the child does so he or she receives a marker to symbolize 1 point scored.

4. If a child cannot make a word, the child waits and hopes the next deal will be better.

5. The cards are collected, shuffled and redealt. Then the same procedure is followed.

6. The child with the most markers at the end of the game is the winner.

Punch Out

purpose: to recall visual elements (digraphs)
materials: an oaktag shape (e.g., doll, football, apple, tree, etc.), pencil and hole punch
procedure:
1. The teacher makes a large oaktag shape with words written around the border of the shape with digraphs punched out.

2. Several different digraph punch-outs can be made.

Example:

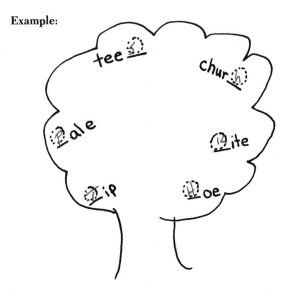

3. This activity is designed for 2 children.
4. One child looks at the front of the shape, inserts the pencil through a hole and identifies the missing digraph and the word.
5. The second child checks the response. (The correct answer is printed on the reverse side adjacent to each hole.)
6. The activity continues.

6   auditory perception: identifying similar sounds

Auditory perception is the ability to hear and identify like sounds. The materials in this chapter provide instruction and practice in identifying sameness in sound and require the student to listen to various phonetic elements, perceive likeness in sound, and repeat the sound either in its original or a modified form.

The activities that follow will assist the student in developing auditory perception acuity, an ability so important to effective reading. Follow-up reinforcement worksheets are provided to supplement the instructional program.

Stand Up, Sit Down

purpose: to identify like sounds
materials: tape recorder and tape
procedure:

1. The teacher previously has tape recorded several pairs of words. (Some have the same phonetic element and some do not.)

Example:	let	let
	fish	fish
	in	out
	snow	snow
	cup	cut

2. The teacher presents the tape to the class. He or she turns on the recorder and the children listen carefully.

3. If the recorded word pairs are alike (e.g., red, red), the children *stand up*. If the word pairs are not alike then the children *sit down*.

4. The activity continues until the tape ends.

5. This activity can be done independently with the children operating the recorder.

Tick-Tock

purpose   to listen and locate sound
materials: a clock
procedure:

1. The teacher brings a loud, ticking clock to school.

2. The children close their eyes while the teacher hides the clock.

3. The children listen carefully, then open their eyes. One of the children tries to locate the clock by pointing to the area in the room from which he or she thinks the ticking sound is coming.

variations:

1. Have 1 child make a sound somewhere in the room while the other children listen with eyes closed. The children open their eyes and the teacher asks, "Who can find the sound?" Have the child say, "I hear the sound. It is_____." (The child must identify the sound (i.e., a "moo" sound or a crying sound, etc.).

2. Have the children look around the room to find things that make sounds. The teacher asks questions such as, "Can you find something that makes a sound if you bounce it?" "Toss it?" "Roll it?" "Jiggle it?" "Drop it?" "Squeeze it?"

Echo?

purpose: to recognize and repeat the same sound
materials: an oral activity
procedure:

1. The teacher stands with his or her back to the class and sings or says something in which a child's name is used.

2. The child whose name the teacher used then echoes back what he or she heard. The child tries to repeat the sentence using the same tone as the teacher.

> **Example:**   Sally Smith has on a red dress. (The child repeats the identical sentence using the same voice tone, inflection, etc.)

Alphabet Sequence

purpose: to identify alphabetical letters and related words orally
materials: an oral activity

procedure:
1. The children sit in a circle.
2. The game starts by the teacher stating that they are going on a trip by boat and each child must take something along that begins with a letter of the alphabet in sequence.
3. Therefore, the first child might say, "My boat is loaded with apples." The next child might say, "My boat is loaded with bananas." The next child could say, "My boat is loaded with cabbage."
4. The game continues until all letters of the alphabet have been used or until someone cannot provide a word.

Roll the Ball

purpose: to identify the same ending elements (rhyming)
materials: a ball
procedure:
1. The children sit in a circle with 1 child in the center.
2. The child in the center says a word (e.g., "cat"), then rolls the ball to someone in the circle.
3. The child who receives the ball must say a rhyming word (e.g., "bat"), then rolls the ball to another child in the circle.
4. The activity continues until no one can think of any more words to rhyme with "cat."
5. The ball goes back to the person in the center who identifies another word, and the same procedure continues.

Rhyme Time

purpose: to identify the same ending elements (rhyming)
materials: oaktag, Magic Marker, paper clips, word cards (consisting of rhyming words) and worksheet (See page 104.)
procedure:
1. The teacher draws a large clock face on a large piece of oaktag. He or she inserts paper clips next to each number on the clock. (The paper clips will be used to hold the word cards.)
2. The teacher announces it's "Rhyme Time," and the game begins.
3. The children sit facing the clock and watch carefully as the teacher inserts a word card next to each number.
4. The children look carefully. The children take turns and remove 2 cards that rhyme from the clock.
5. The game continues until all cards are removed.

Worksheet

Directions: Circle the pictures that rhyme in each row.

Example:

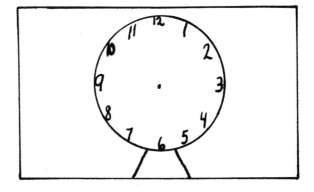

6. The children count up their pairs, and the child with the most pairs is the winner.

7. The teacher can put up a new set of cards, and the game continues.

Climb the Mountain

purpose: to identify the same beginning consonants
materials: chalkboard, chalk and word cards
procedure:
  1. The teacher draws a large mountain on the chalkboard with a number of lines at various intervals to signify steps.

Example:

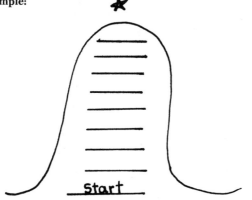

  2. The teacher holds up a word card (e.g., *bat*).

  3. Then the teacher says a sentence that contains the same phonetic element as the key word.

Example: Bud can't see the bird.

4. The first child in the group repeats the words from the sentence that have the same beginning sound as the key word (e.g., "Bud," "bird").

5. If the child is correct he or she starts to climb the mountain by moving up 1 space. (The child's name is written on the line.)

6. The game continues in the same manner with each child in the group having a turn.

7. The first child to *climb the mountain* successfully is the winner.

Jump the Hurdles

purpose: to identify ending consonant sounds
materials: oaktag game board
procedure:
1. The teacher prepares a game board.

   Example:

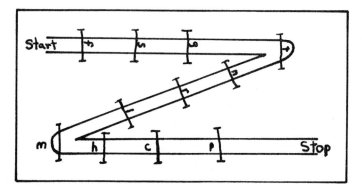

2. The game is played with 2 teams.

3. The first team member starts with the letter next to the first hurdle. The child must say the "f" sound orally and give a word ending with the letter "f." For example, the child might say "leaf." He or she then jumps the first hurdle and continues to the next.

4. If the child can follow the same procedure correctly for each hurdle, 9 points (1 for each hurdle) are scored for his team.

5. If the child correctly jumps only 3 hurdles, then his or her team receives only 3 points, etc.

6. The opposing team member takes his or her turn at jumping hurdles and scoring points.

7. Each person must name different words—no duplicate words allowed.

8. When each team member has had a turn, the total score is tallied.

Mural Fun

purpose: to identify consonant blends
materials: mural paper and picture cards
procedure:
1. The teacher makes a large mural of blends (or whatever skill is being reinforced) and places the mural on the floor.

Example:

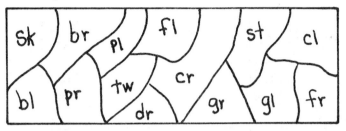

2. The picture cards are placed in a pile near the mural.
3. The child chooses a picture card, says its name, and then places the picture on its correct space on the mural.
4. The child repeats this procedure until the mural is covered.
5. The child may time him or herself at this activity and even compare timing with a friend.

Horseshoe Game

purpose: to identify beginning blends and digraphs
materials: oaktag game board, Magic Markers, 1 die and markers
procedure:
1. The teacher makes a large horseshoe-shape game with pictures drawn at regular intervals.
2. The first player rolls the die.
3. The player counts off from start and moves his or her marker the number of spaces indicated on the die.
4. Where the player lands, he or she must name the board picture and 1 other word with the same beginning blend or digraph.
5. If the player is unable to give a word with the same beginning blend or digraph, he or she must move back 1 space and give the name of the picture and 1 other word with the same beginning blend or

digraph. The player continues in this fashion until a beginning sound match is made.

6. The player who reaches *Stop* first is the winner.

   Example:

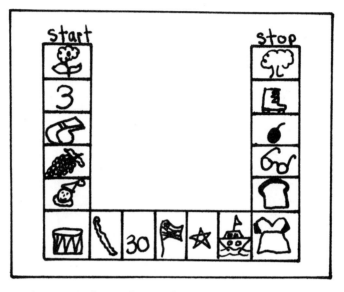

This is a good game for 3-8 players.

Chalk It Up

purpose: to identify consonants, blends, digraphs and vowels
materials: chalk and sidewalk or blacktop area
procedure:

1. A large hopscotch game is drawn with chalk on an outside cement or blacktop surface.

   Example:

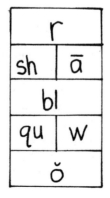

2. The child throws a stone into a box. The child must identify the sound and give a word that contains that sound. The child then hops to retrieve the stone.
3. The game continues until each child has had a turn.
4. Each child continues to play until he or she no longer can identify the sound or name a corresponding word.

See Double

purpose: to identify the same double middle consonants
materials: game board, word cards (all containing double consonants in the middle), paper clips and worksheet (See page 110.)
procedure:
1. The teacher prepares a game board.

   Example:

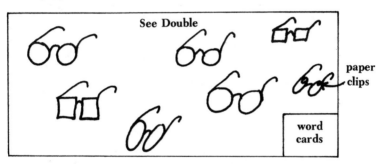

2. A child sorts through the word cards and finds a pair of words that contain the same double middle consonants.

3. When a pair has been found, the child hooks the match on a pair of glasses on the game board.

   Example:

4. The child continues to sort through the cards and fills in the game board.

5. When the game board is completed, the child takes the board to the teacher for checking and also attempts to read the words.

Worksheet

Directions: Choose from nn, pp, ll, tt, dd.

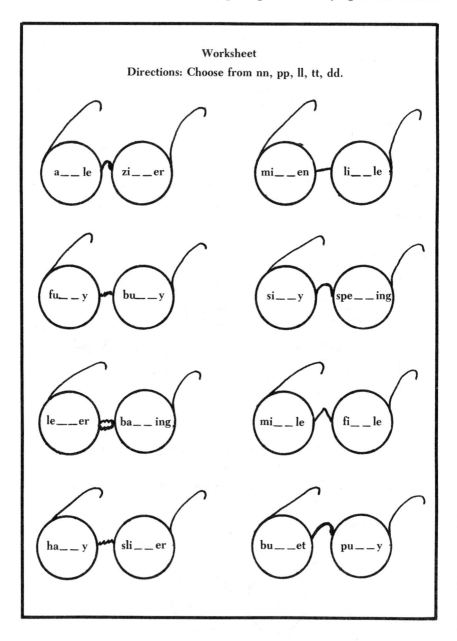

a__ le   zi___er   mi__en   li__le

fu___y   bu___y   si__y   spe__ing

le___er   ba__ing   mi__le   fi__le

ha___y   sli__er   bu__et   pu__y

6. The teacher then gives the child a worksheet. The child must choose the correct double middle consonant and write it in the blank space.

Cover-Up!

purpose: to identify beginning, middle and ending sounds
materials: oaktag, Magic Marker and markers
procedure:
1. The teacher makes several oaktag game boards with related questions under the grid.

Example:

2. The teacher displays 1 game board at a time.

3. The first child in the group reads the first sentence and tries to identify the sound. If it is correct he or she places a marker over it and says "Cover-Up!"

4. If the child is incorrect, someone else in the group gets a try at it.

5. The game then continues with each child taking a turn and until all the sounds are covered.

6. The teacher then may try the childrens' skills at another cover-up game.

7 auditory discrimination: hearing differences in sounds

In Chapter 6 the ability to identify similarity in phonetic elements was covered. Auditory discrimination is the ability to listen and identify *differences* in phonetic elements. Just as being able to discern likeness in sound is important to effective reading, the ability to discriminate is equally critical.

The activities in this chapter require oral, written and drawn responses; they also employ rhyming words, vowel sounds and other sound patterns.

Name That Sound

purpose: to combine auditory images with visual images
materials: record player, a record of different sounds and picture cards
procedure:
1. The teacher plays a record of sounds found in the home, school, farm, neighborhood and zoo. (*Note:* Scott, Foresman & Co. has produced a very good record of such sounds, entitled *Sounds I Hear.*)

2. The children gather around the record player and listen carefully as the teacher plays the record.

3. The children listen to the record, visualize the sounds and identify the object making the sound from the picture cards.

4. This activity also can be used to develop sequencing skills.

variation: a record entitled *The Lonesome House*, by Douglas Moore and Henry Brent, might be used. The teacher tells the children to close their eyes and imagine all the sounds they would hear if they were alone in the house. Afterwards, the children are given paper and crayons and instructed to draw all the things they could visualize.

Draw and Display

purpose: to identify the different sounds we hear
materials: drawing paper and crayons
procedure:
1. The teacher and the children take a walk around the school.
2. When they have returned to the classroom, the various sounds are discussed.
3. The teacher identifies 1 sound, and the children draw a picture about it.
4. When all children have their pictures completed, they share them with the other children so that they may see the differences in interpretation.
5. The teacher then may identify another sound, and the same procedure continues.

What Is It?

purpose: to identify the different sounds we hear
materials: an oral activity
procedure:
1. The children are asked to close their eyes and listen.
2. The teacher makes various sounds, and the children must be able to identify the sounds.

> **Example:**   Tapping on the floor
>
> Crying
>
> Ringing a bell
>
> Opening a door
>
> Opening a window
>
> Chalk on chalkboard
>
> Whistling
>
> Clapping
>
> Sliding a chair
>
> Turning on the water

Tray Treat

purpose: to identify sounds we hear

materials: a tray and a variety of objects (e.g., a whistle, measuring spoons, marbles, keys and straight pins)

procedure:

1. The teacher shows the children the collection of articles on a tray.

2. The children look carefully at the tray; then the teacher removes the tray from their view.

3. The children close their eyes, and the teacher makes a sound with 1 of the objects.

4. The children must be able to tell what object matches the sound.

5. The same procedure continues with each one of the objects displayed on the tray.

One, Two, Three, Four

purpose: to identify rhyming words

materials: word cards containing 1 rhyming word on each card in sets of 1, 2, 3 or 4.

Example:

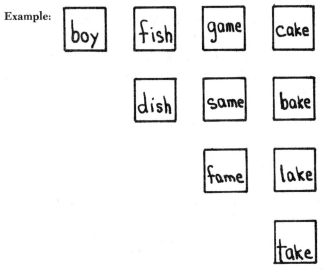

procedure:

1. The teacher shuffles the rhyming word cards and then spreads them out face-up on the table.

2. The children, in turn, find matching pairs, triplets, or even quadruplets of rhyming words (initially by identifying the words orally and then matching them correctly.)

The End

purpose: to identify specific phonetic endings
materials: word cards and construction paper tails (counters)

Example:

procedure:
1. The child listens as the teacher says a word containing a specific phonetic ending element.
2. The child then chooses 6 word cards from the teacher and reads them silently.
3. The child must choose and show the teacher only those word cards that end the same as the key word mentioned.
4. For every correct match the child receives a tail as a reward.
5. At the end of the game the tails are counted and then collected by the teacher.

Around We Go

purpose: to identify ending consonant sounds
materials: chalkboard and chalk
procedure:
1. The teacher draws a large circle on the board and surrounds the circle with consonant letters.

Example:

2. Each player takes a turn at attempting to make it around the circle.
3. The player, starting at any point on the circle, must give a word that ends with the designated letter. If he or she is correct, the child goes to the next sound (clockwise or counter-clockwise).
4. If the child is incorrect, he or she loses a turn.
5. The first child to make it successfully around is the winner. The remaining children also should finish the game.

Beginning, Middle, End

purpose: to identify a particular sound appearing at the beginning, middle or end of a word
materials: construction paper, scissors and glue
procedure:
1. The teacher makes 3 cone-shaped hats from construction paper. The hats should depict the head, body and tail of an animal.

> **Example:**

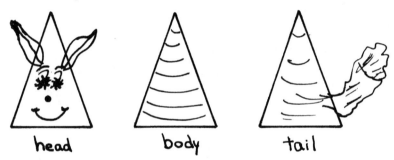

head   body   tail

2. The game starts off with 3 children wearing the hats.
3. The teacher identifies a certain sound to be reviewed (e.g., *d*).
4. The teacher proceeds to mention related *d* words.
5. If the teacher mentions a word with the sound at the beginning, the child wearing the head hat stands up. If the teacher mentions a word with the sound in the middle, the body hat stands up, etc.
6. The children in the group take turns wearing the hats, and the game continues.

Clown Around

purpose: to identify long and short vowels
materials: a large clown made from oaktag paper and word cards

Example:

procedure:
1. This is a good activity for any number of children.
2. The children take a card from the word bag.
3. The children look at the underlined vowel.
4. The children place the card in the correct pocket.
5. When all word cards have been dispersed, the cards can be self-checked. (Whether the vowel is long or short should be indicated on the back of the card.)

Make a Poster

purpose: to identify vowel sounds
materials: manila paper, Magic Marker, magazines, scissors and paste
procedure:
1. Each child is given a piece of sectioned paper with a key vowel word written in each box.

Example:

căt	bĕd	pĭg	hŏt	sŭn
cāke	trēe	pīe	cōat	mūsic

2. The children are given a magazine and are encouraged to complete their vowel posters by cutting and pasting pictures in the appropriate boxes.

3. When completed, the childrens' vowel posters can be displayed in the classroom.

Sound Off

purpose: to identify the vowel sounds
materials: oaktag paper, clear contact paper, Magic Marker, grease pencil and word cards
procedure:
1. The teacher makes several oaktag game cards containing the vowel sounds. The game cards are covered with clear contact paper.

Example:

Sound Off	a	e	i	o	u
Long					
Short					

2. The teacher dictates a word, holds up a word card containing the same word, and the child writes the word in the appropriate box.
3. The teacher continues to *sound off* until all the spaces are filled in.
4. In this game, everyone should be a winner if the vowel sound is identified correctly. (The teacher is handy for on-the-spot checking.)
5. When the game is completed, the grease pencil words can be wiped off easily with a cloth or tissue paper, and the cards are ready to be used again.

Wall-to-Wall Blends

purpose: to identify blends
materials: bulletin board, construction paper, Magic Marker, word cards, crayons, magazines and paper clips
procedure:
1. The teacher makes the entire bulletin board into a large blend-board.

Example:

tr	cl	sw	pr	cr
bl	dr	br	fr	pl
tw	gr	fl	sk	sn

2. Each child is given a certain number of word cards. The teacher says a word, and each child finds the correct blend from his or her cards and pins the card over the blend on the blend-board. The first child to pin up all of his or her word cards is the winner.

variations:

1. The children can cut out magazine pictures and paste them in the correct box.

2. The children may draw and color pictures in the boxes.

3. Paper clips can be attached to each section, and the children can clip appropriate pictures or word cards to appropriate sections.

4. An envelope can be glued to each section, and the children can fill the envelope with blend items.

Dialects

purpose: to recognize differences in speech pattern (dialect)
materials: an oral activity
procedure:

1. The teacher reads poems or parts of stories containing different dialects so that the children can hear the differences in speech pattern.

   Example: *Irish:* Sean O'Casey;
                   English: Sherlock Holmes, etc.

2. The children listen as the teacher reads and pay particular attention to the different kinds of speech.

3. After listening to the story or poem, the children discuss the differences in the speech.

Color Me

purpose: to identify color words and their beginning sounds
materials: crayons and worksheet (See page 121.)
procedure:

1. The teacher plays a game with color words.

2. The teacher mentions a color word and 2 other similar words (e.g., red, bed, said).

3. The children are to listen carefully and repeat the 2 words that are not colors.

4. The same procedure continues with other color words.

5. A worksheet containing short stories is given to each child.

Worksheet

A boy named Ralph
had a new racing car.
The racing car was
a bright red color.

The bright yellow
sun was so hot it
would make your yo-yo
melt.

Mother sent William
shopping for milk.
William was wearing his
new white shoes. But his
shoes weren't white when
he got home. What happened?

Mother and Bob went
shopping for a new toy
boat. Bob found a
nice one. It was
big and blue.

"Have you ever seen a
purple pig?" said Paul.
Purple pigs are purple
because they eat plums.

6. The child is to read each story, locate the color word and underline it with the correct colored crayon.

7. Then the child proceeds to find other words in the story that begin with the same letter and underlines these with the same color.

    Example: The clouds are <u>black</u>.

                 "I think it's going to rain," said <u>Bob</u>.

8   visual recognition activities

Visual recognition is the ability to *see* and identify likeness in letters, phonetic elements, words, etc. The materials in this chapter provide significant practice in this vital area of reading, cover a wide variety of concepts (i.e., vowels, blends, consonants, etc.), assist the student in perceiving sameness in phonetic elements visually, and supply valuable reinforcement for this essential reading ingredient.

'Tis the Season

purpose: to match season-related activities to the correct season
materials: 4 large pictures (representing the seasons), and a set of small pictures (season-related)
procedure:
1. The teacher places the 4 large season pictures on the chalk ledge.
2. The small picture cards are distributed to the children.
3. In turn, the children are to match the small pictures with the large ones by placing the smaller pictures on the chalk ledge next to the correct season.

Likeness

purpose: to identify the likeness in objects
materials: classroom objects
procedure:
1. The teacher holds up something for all the children to see and describes the object.

    Example: "I am holding a yardstick."

2. The children are asked to find something else that is similar in some way.

Example: "I am holding a ruler."

3. The teacher has the child explain why the particular item was selected.

4. The game continues with the teacher selecting another object.

5. Similar objects could include the following:

> Clock—watch
> Flashlight—ceiling light
> Chalk—pencil
> Hand eraser—rubber eraser

Eye-See

purpose: to identify words visually that contain the same phonetic elements

materials: oaktag paper, paper clips and word cards

procedure:

1. The teacher makes a large eye from oaktag paper and inserts paper clips (to hold word cards) at various intervals.

Example:

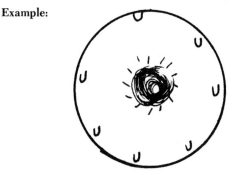

2. The teacher displays a number of word cards on the chalk ledge.

3. The child responds by picking out the words that are the same and places them on the "eye."

4. The same procedure continues with the other children in the group.

Crossword Puzzle

purpose: to identify the number of phonetic elements in a word visually

materials: pencil and worksheet (See page 125.)

procedure:

1. The teacher reviews vocabulary words with a group of children and then gives the children a follow-up worksheet containing some of the words.

Worksheet

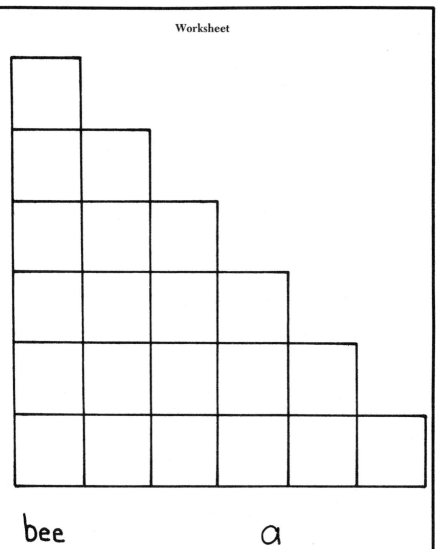

bee   a

better   me

stand   tree

2. The children are to identify the words and then find the right row in which to write the words.

3. There should be just enough boxes in each row for the letters of 1 word.

What's My Position?

purpose: to identify the same phonetic elements visually
materials: oaktag flowers, word cards and a bulletin board
procedure:
1. The teacher displays a flower garden of sounds on a bulletin board.

Example:

2. The teacher shows the children a word containing a specific letter or letters (consonant, blend or digraph) in the initial or final position.

Example:

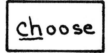

3. The children are to decide to which flower the word card belongs and then insert the card in the correct slit corresponding to its position (initial or final).

4. The game continues until all the word cards have been placed properly.

Ads, Ads, Ads

purpose: to identify visually sounds that are the same
materials: manila paper, magazines, scissors, paste and pencil

procedure:
1. The children are given paper, a magazine, scissors and paste.
2. The children cut several ads from the magazine and paste them on their papers.
3. The children underline the sounds that are the same in each add.

      Example: You've come a long way baby.

                  It's the real thing.

                  Eat smart, stay in the pink.

                  Meet the sweetest family ever.

Picture This!

purpose: to recognize and identify beginning consonants
materials: manila paper (cut to fit inside booklets the teacher makes), magazines, scissors, paste and stapler
procedure:
1. The teacher prepares booklets to represent the sounds to be reviewed.

      Example:

2. The children receive paper, a magazine, scissors and paste. They are to cut out pictures and/or words to paste on their papers to correlate with the booklets the teacher made. (The children should be permitted to do as many pages as possible.)

      Example:

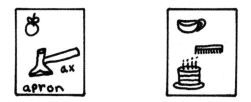

3. When the childrens' pages are completed, the teacher staples the booklets together. Each booklet should contain only 1 sound (e.g.,

the *a* booklet should contain all the childrens' pages containing *a* pictures or words).

Word Bank Activity

purpose: to identify the same phonetic element visually (beginning or ending sounds)

materials: picture-word cards and individual word banks for each child

procedure:
1. The teacher holds up a picture-word card.

   Example:

2. Using this as the key, the children use words from their word banks to find those that begin (or end) like the key word.

variation: this activity can be made into a race to see which child can display his or her words first, or to see which child can display the most within a given period of time.

Paper Bag Sounds

purpose: to identify beginning sounds visually

materials: a decorated paper bag and small objects

procedure:
1. The teacher fills a large bag with labeled objects beginning with various sounds.
2. The instructions for the activity are written on the bag.
3. The children are directed to examine the contents of the bag and match the objects beginning with the same sound (e.g., all the objects beginning with *b*).

Card Match

purpose: to identify ending sounds visually

materials: picture-word cards and letter cards

procedure:
1. This is a good game for 2 children.

2. All the cards are shuffled together and placed in 1 pile.
3. The first child draws a card and places it face up in front of him or herself.

   Example: 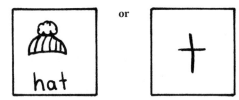 or

4. The other child draws a card. If the card drawn matches the first card in sound or ending letter, the second child retrieves the first card and gets to keep both.
5. If the second child to draw does not make a match, he or she places the card face up in front of him or her, and the game continues with the first child again drawing and trying to make a match with the first card or second card drawn, etc.
6. The game continues with the children matching picture-word cards and letter cards.
7. Only the person drawing is in a position to make a match.

Peek-a-Boo House

purpose: to identify blends and digraphs visually
materials: oaktag paper, brass fasteners and Magic Marker
procedure:
1. The teacher makes a house from oaktag paper and cuts 2 window openings in the front of the house.

   Example:

2. The teacher makes a word wheel and a related sound wheel.

   Example:

3. The wheels are attached to the house with brass fasteners so that when the wheel is rotated, the outside edge of the wheel appears in the window.

Example:

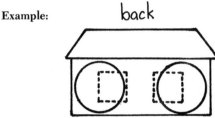

4. Several peek-a-boo houses can be made, and the children can dial a word and its corresponding sound independently.

Example:

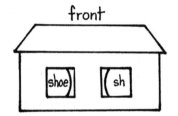

If the Shoe Fits, Wear It

purpose: to identify the same phonetic element visually (blends)
materials: construction paper shoes and shoebox
procedure:
  1. The teacher writes a word on 1 shoe and its blend on another.

Example:

2. All the shoes are placed in the shoebox.
3. The child takes the box, sorts through the shoes, and attempts to match pairs (the word and its blend).
4. The shoes can be made in different configurations so that the child does not match a word and its blend from the outline of the shoe.

variation: before school, tape a word and/or sound on the shoe of each child as they arrive. The children then must find partners with a corresponding word and/or sound.

Number-O

purpose: to identify beginning sounds
materials: pocket chart, word cards, letter cards, chalkboard and chalk
procedure:
1. The teacher places word cards and letter cards in the pocket chart.

Example:

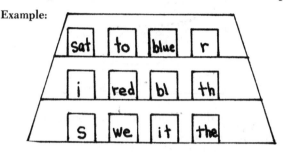

2. The teacher writes a number (e.g., 3) on the chalkboard.
3. The first child removes that number of word cards and corresponding beginning letter cards.
4. The child identifies the beginning sound and then reads the word.
5. The teacher changes the number and the next child participates.

Find the Hidden Word

purpose: to identify beginning consonants visually
materials: basal readers, chalkboard and chalk
procedure:
1. The children are given their basal readers.
2. The teacher writes a consonant on the board (e.g., "w") and directs the children to find the "w" words on a certain page and paragraph in their readers.
3. In turn, the children mention all the "w" words they can find and read.
4. The same procedure continues with other consonant sounds.

Branch Out

purpose: to identify beginning sounds and words
materials: oaktag paper, a die, Magic Marker and markers

procedure:
1. The teacher makes a branch-out game board consisting of vocabulary words and spaces for penalties and rewards written at regular intervals.

Example:

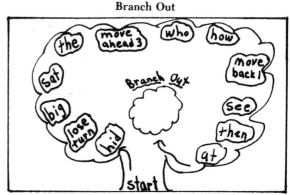

2. Each player tosses the die and moves the number of indicated spaces.
3. The child must identify the beginning sound and then read the word on which he or she lands.
4. If the child is unable to identify the sound or read the word, he must return to his original space.
5. The first child to reach the *Branch Out* space is the winner.

Hairy Vowels

purpose: to identify long and short vowels visually
materials: chalkboard, chalk and worksheet (See page 133.)
procedure:
1. The teacher draws a large rabbit on the board with vowel sounds written on it.

Example:

Worksheet

2. The children orally identify the sounds and then give related words.
3. The teacher writes the words on the rabbit in the appropriate spaces.
4. The children then are given follow-up worksheets and their readers.
5. The children are to locate specific vowel words in their books and write the words on the rabbit in the appropriate spaces.

Wheel and Deal

purpose: to recognize and identify vowel sounds visually
materials: oaktag paper, construction paper and brass fasteners
procedure:

1. The teacher makes a large, oaktag paper clown face with a slit cut out to represent the clown's mouth. A word wheel and vowel wheel are also made.

    Example:

2. The wheels are attached to the clown with brass fasteners so that the words and vowels on the wheels can be seen through the clown's mouth.

    Example:

    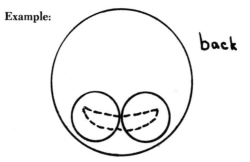

3. The child is given the clown and is to spin the wheels to make a match.

Example:

4. The teacher should be handy for checking.

5. Then the clown is given to another child in the group, and that child gets to *wheel* a match and *deals* the clown to someone else.

Ring It

purpose: to identify vowel sounds visually

materials: shower curtain rings and word cards (with a hole punched in each)

procedure:

1. The teacher writes a vowel sound on the board (e.g., "ō").

2. Then the teacher distributes an equal number of word cards to each player.

3. Each child looks at his or her word cards and identifies those that contain the long "o" sound.

4. Each child strings the long "o" cards onto a shower ring.

5. The teacher checks for correct cards, and incorrect cards are discarded.

6. The player with the most cards on his or her ring is the winner.

7. The same procedure continues with another vowel sound.

9   practicing visual discrimination

Unlike "visual recognition," which focuses on recognizing similarity, "visual discrimination" provides practice in recognizing differences in letters, words and phonetic elements. Moreover, this chapter covers the concepts of size and shape and such difficult areas for students as the difference between "b" and "d." As in the previous chapters, follow-up materials are provided to assist in review, reinforcement and mastery of this important aspect of reading.

Build-a-Letter

purpose: to identify letters of the alphabet
materials: tag board, Magic Markers, scissors, envelope, a decorated box
procedure:
1. Make several large, tag board squares with letter parts drawn on with a Magic Marker. (Make 2 sets—capital and small.)

   Example:

2. Make the matching missing letter parts from tag board and store in the envelope.
3. The child takes a letter part from the envelope and matches it with the correct letter card.

   Example:

4. If the child uses all the pieces from the envelope and has 2 complete alphabet sets (capital and small), he or she has mastered the skill.

5. The completed activity is stored in a brightly decorated box.

The Dinner Table

purpose: to identify and correlate shapes

materials: a solid-colored paper tablecloth with drawn outlines of various dinner objects, cut-out drawings of table objects and a decorated box

Example:

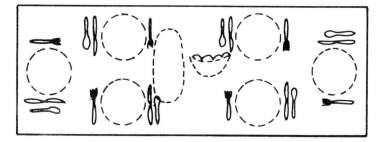

procedure:

1. Spread the tablecloth out on the floor or on a table.

2. Have a child reach into the decorated box and draw out a cut-out and place it on its corresponding shape on the table.

Example:

3. Give each child a turn until the dinner table is all set.

4. The dinner cut-outs can be labeled to establish a word-symbol relationship:

Example:

In the Box

purpose: to develop a child's ability to estimate size

materials: old workbook pictures (various sizes), index cards, scissors, glue, Magic Markers, clear contact paper and a storage box

procedure:
1. Glue workbook pictures on the index cards and cover with contact paper.
2. On index cards draw pictures of variously shaped boxes that would accommodate the items in your picture collection.
3. Place the index cards containing pictures and box shapes in the game box.
4. The child sorts through the various index cards and must match a picture card with the correct size box cards.
5. The picture cards can be coded to correspond to the correct box card for self-checking.

Example:

Odd Man Out

purpose: to discriminate between letters
materials: letter cards, word cards, pocket chart, shoebox, construction paper, scissors and glue
procedure:
1. Make an "Odd Man" box.

Example: a slit on top

2. Place a series of three letters in the pocket chart (*d, r, d*).

3. The children look carefully for the "Odd Man Out" and then proceed to place the "Odd Man" in the decorated shoebox.

4. This activity may be increased to display 4 or 5 or more letters in the pocket chart.

5. You also may show a group of 3 words (*cat, cat, cut*) and have the children find the "Odd Man Out."

6. The letters and word cards can all be stored in the "Odd Man" box.

Smile or Frown

purpose: to discriminate between like and different word pairs
materials: word cards (some identical pairs and others, different pairs) and an oaktag game board set up as follows:

procedure:

1. The word cards are placed face down in a pile.

2. The child draws a card from the top of the pile.

   Example: | bed | bed | the child decides if the pair is alike or different.

3. If the pair is alike, it is placed in the column under the smile face.

4. If the drawn card contains a pair that is different, then the card is placed in the frown column.

   Example: | sit | sat |

5. The child scores a point for each correct match.

6. The word cards are coded on the back (☺ ☹) for self-grading.

The Line-Up

purpose: to identify beginning sounds

materials: word cards, storage box or envelope for cards and oaktag game board set up as follows:

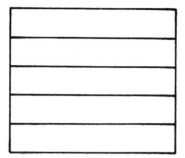

procedure:

1. The child sorts through the word cards and matches beginning sounds.

2. The first row on the game board is lined with cards of the same beginning sound. The second row is lined with cards all beginning with a different first sound, etc.

> **Example:**   First row: *cat, cup, cot, cash*
>
> Second row: *tree, tip, time, tea*

3. The child may time him or herself to see how long it takes to classify the sounds.

Tempera Match

purpose: to match letters, words, phrases and sentences
materials: blackboard, chalk, tempera paint and brush
procedure:

1. On the board, display an activity in which a child matches letters, words, phrases and sentences.

> **Examples:**

g R		sit but		said
z G		was sit		to
a A		are are		this
r Z		but was		we
				this

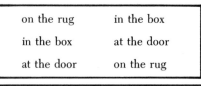

on the rug	in the box
in the box	at the door
at the door	on the rug

Did you see the bear? Did you see the beaver run?

Did you see the beaver run? Did you see the bear?

2. The child makes his or her selection by using a brush and tempera paint and matches letters, words, etc., as follows:

3. This is a very colorful activity for the child to engage in, and the paint washes off the board with ease.

Which One?

purpose: to identify objects and sounds
materials: flannel board and flannel cut-outs
procedure:
1. Place 3 or 4 flannel objects on the board and have the children identify the object and its beginning sound (or whatever phonetic skill is being reinforced).

   Example:

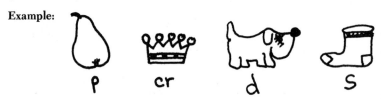

2. Then have the children close their eyes while the teacher removes 1 object.
3. The children open their eyes and try to identify the missing flannel object and its sound.
4. For a challenge, the teacher may try to remove 2 or more objects.

Go!

purpose: to identify like letters and words and their respective sounds

materials: a series of matching cards with words and/or letters on them

    Example:

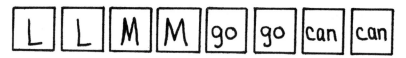

procedure:
1. A dealer shuffles the cards and deals all the cards to 2 players.
2. The cards are placed face down in front of each player.
3. At the sound of *Go!* from the dealer, each child turns up 1 card simultaneously.
4. If the cards match, the child saying the word (or letter or sound) first claims the cards and the game goes on.
5. If the cards do not match, the players continue to turn up subsequent cards at the sound of *Go!*
6. The winner is the child who receives the largest number of cards.

A Shady Deal

purpose: to identify beginning sounds

materials: a window shade, old workbook pictures, metal discs, jiffy picture hangers and storage box for discs

procedure:
1. The picture hangers are attached (lick-and-stick) to the window shade with consonant sounds written on them.

    Example:

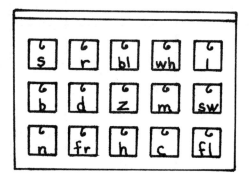

    The shade is tacked to a bulletin board.

2. The workbook pictures are mounted on the metal discs.
3. The picture discs are placed face down on the table.
4. The teacher deals 1 disc at a time to a child.

5. The child must match his or her pictured disc to its corresponding sound indicated on the jiffy picture hanger. The disc then is hung on the shade.
6. The child receives 1 point for every disc he or she correctly matches.
7. The window shade is rolled up easily and stored.

Bed Time

purpose: to discriminate between the letters *b* and *d*
materials: chalkboard, chalk, magazines, scissors, paste and worksheet (See page 145.)
procedure:
1. On the chalkboard make b d.
2. Tell the following bed time story: "It is time for_____ (child's name) to go to bed. You will lie down and place your head on the b̲ part of the bed (draw the child's head on the b̲). The b̲ is really your pillow. The d̲ is at the foot of the bed and you will rest your feet on the d̲." (Draw the rest of the child with his or her feet resting on the d̲.)

   Example:

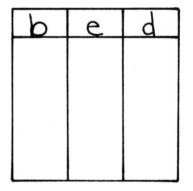

3. The children then receive a follow-up worksheet:

   Example:

b	e	d

4. The children are to use magazines and find words that have the *b, e,* and *d* sounds, cut them out and paste them in the correct column.
5. The children may draw themselves in bed on their worksheets, and then the completed lesson may be displayed somewhere in the room.

Buckets of Blends

purpose: to identify blends
materials: construction paper, magazines, scissors, glue and Magic Marker
procedure:
1. The teacher makes several buckets with blends written on them. The buckets are displayed on a bulletin board.

     Example:

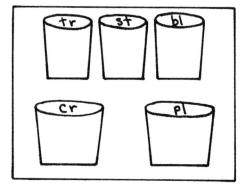

2. The children are given magazines and are to find pictures that correspond to the correct blend, or they may find words that contain the blends.
3. This is an activity that can be worked on daily. When a bucket becomes too full, the teacher can take it down and put up a different blend bucket.

Class Action

purpose: to match phrases and objects
materials: classroom phrases and a decorated box

     Examples for phrases:

The toys are in a box.	The chalk is on the chalk ledge.
The book is on the shelf.	The flowers are by the window.
The bell is on the desk.	The ball is in the corner.

practicing visual discrimination

procedure:
1. The phrase cards are placed in a box.
2. The class is divided into teams and the first team member card from the box.
3. He or she reads the card and matches and places it near the classroom object.
4. For every correctly read and matched phrase, the team receives 1 point.
5. The team with the most points at the end of the game is the winner.

Long and Short Racing Fun

purpose: to identify long and short vowel sounds
materials: oaktag game board and envelopes containing word cards (The game board is made to look like a race track with start, finish and pitstops.)

Example:

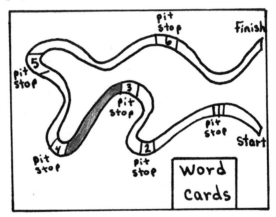

procedure:
1. Each child makes a racing car out of construction paper and places his or her name on it.
2. Each child begins at *Start* and draws a word card from the envelope, reads the word and identifies its long or short vowel sound.
3. If the child incorrectly identifies the vowel sound he loses his turn; on the other hand, if he correctly identifies the sound he then proceeds to the first pit stop. He stops there until the other participants have all had their turns.
4. The first person to reach the finish line is the winner.

Flower Power

purpose: to identify long and short vowels
materials: oaktag game board, word cards, markers and pictures representing the long and short vowel sounds
The game board should be set up as follows:

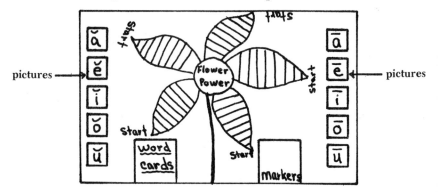

procedure:
1. Each student is given a marker.
2. The student then draws a card from the word card envelope.
3. The child must say the printed word correctly and identify its vowel sound. (The picture key along the side of the game board is an aid when a child is having difficulty.)
4. If the child is correct, he moves 1 space on his petal. If he is incorrect, he remains where he is.
5. The first child to reach the center of the flower is the *Flower Power Champ.*

Anagram

purpose: to identify known words and their proper spellings
materials: blackboard and chalk
procedure:
1. Place many rearranged words on the chalkboard.
2. When a child identifies a word, he or she circles it and rewrites the word within the circle. The child then initials his or her work.

Example: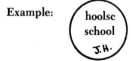

3. The child with the most initialed circles is the winner.
4. Choice of words can be based on the child's vocabulary, class list, or based on a theme (e.g., animals, cars, food, etc.).

10 vocabulary exercises for children

The following materials are successful techniques that may be employed to build, develop and strengthen a child's vocabulary. The activities may be used to introduce new words and familiarize, classify and reinforce old words.

To this end, a number of games are provided that utilize a variety of different methods (e.g., sight and word cards, etc.), all intended to stimulate student interest and learning. Follow-up activities also are provided to ensure maximum review and reinforcement.

Vocabulary Building Game

purpose: to review and reinforce a child's vocabulary
materials: an oral activity
procedure:
1. The children are arranged in a circle.
2. The teacher asks each child a question such as, "What is a baby cow called?" or "What does a ball do when you drop it?" or "What does an angry bear say?"
3. If a child cannot answer a question, he or she moves outside the circle.
4. The winner is the child who remains in the circle the longest.

Strike!

purpose: to identify vocabulary words
materials: oaktag paper, construction paper bowling pins (displaying more difficult vocabulary words), construction paper duck pins (displaying easier vocabulary words) and paper clips
procedure:
1. The teacher makes an oaktag game board by cutting slits in the oaktag and inserting paper clips in each slit to hold the bowling pins and duck pins.

Example:

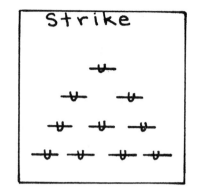

2. The teacher inserts the bowling pins or the duck pins onto the game board.

3. For a child to make a strike, he or she must read each vocabulary word correctly.

4. One point is scored for each word read correctly.

5. The children keep track of their own scores.

6. When each child in the group has had a turn, the child with the most points is the winner.

7. The game can be played again by inserting 10 different pins.

Vocabulary Concentration

purpose: to identify identical vocabulary words
materials: word cards (duplicate sets)
procedure:

1. All the word cards are placed face down on the floor (or on a large table) in neat rows.

Example:

2. Each child, in turn, flips over 2 cards and tries to make a match.

3. If the child doesn't make a match, the cards are returned face down to the floor (table).

4. If a match can be made, the player keeps those 2 cards and continues

to draw 2 more cards. A player can continue to draw cards so long as matches are made.

5. The game is over when all cards have been matched, and the child with the most cards is the winner.

Vocabulary Hop

purpose: to review and reinforce vocabulary words
materials: oil cloth, permanent Magic Marker and bean bag
procedure:
1. The teacher makes a hopscotch diagram on a large piece of oil cloth.
2. Various words are written on the diagram.

Example:

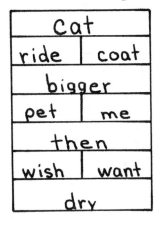

3. The first child throws a bean bag onto a square.
4. The child must hop up to the square, say the word, pick up the bean bag and return.
5. Each child plays until he or she misses.

Go Fish

purpose: to review and reinforce vocabulary words
materials: blue corrugated paper, construction paper, paper clips, fishing pole (pole with string and magnet attached to the string)
procedure:
1. The teacher cuts the corrugated paper to resemble a pond.
2. Many fish shapes are cut from the construction paper, and a paper clip is placed on the nose of the fish.
3. The teacher then writes vocabulary words on the fish, and the fish are placed word down in the pond.

4. The child uses the fishing pole and fishes for construction paper fish.
5. The child must read the word on the fish that he or she catches.
6. For every word read correctly, the child keeps the fish.
7. Each child gets a turn to fish.
8. The child who reads the most words correctly wins the game.

Phonogram Pond

purpose: to match phonetic elements and be able to make words
materials: blue corrugated paper and construction paper fish
procedure:
1. The teacher cuts the corrugated paper to resemble a fish pond.
2. The teacher writes parts of vocabulary words on the fish and the fish are placed in the pond.

Example:

corrugated paper ⟶

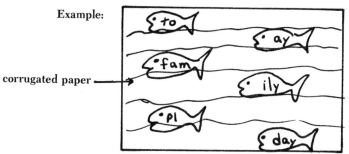

3. The child must match beginning and ending parts and identify the word.

Example:

4. This is a good game for independent review, or it can be played by a group of children.

Blockhead

purpose: to review and reinforce vocabulary words
materials: wooden blocks (2″ × 2″, permanent Magic Markers, construction paper and blockhead pattern (See page 153.)
procedure:
1. The teacher writes vocabulary words on all sides of the wooden blocks.
2. The teacher makes several construction paper heads, hats, ears and neckties, so that when assembled the parts will form a blockhead.

Pattern for Blockhead

head

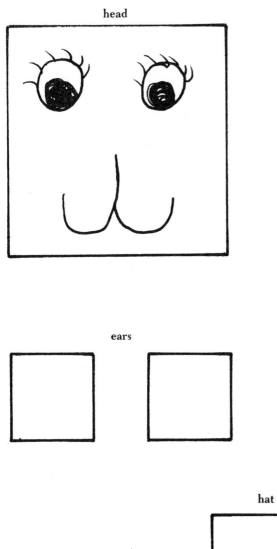

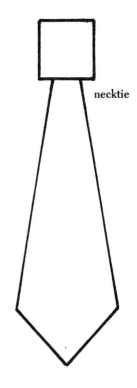

necktie

ears

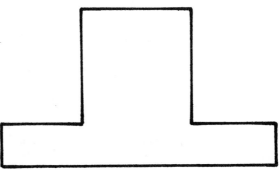

hat

Example:

3. A child rolls the blocks and names as many vocabulary words as he or she can.

4. For each correct vocabulary word identified the child receives a blockhead part. The object of the activity is to get all the parts and make a blockhead.

5. In turn, the children all try to make blockheads.

The Bear Goes Over the Mountain

purpose: to identify sight words and/or phrases
materials: oaktag paper, construction paper, word cards and phrase cards
procedure:
1. The teacher makes an oaktag game board to resemble a mountain. The teacher also makes several different colored bears from construction paper.

Example:

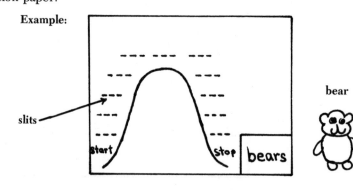

2. The teacher places vocabulary word cards and/or phrase cards in the slits.
3. Each child gets a different colored bear as his or her marker.
4. Each child gets a chance to go up and over the mountain by reading the card successfully.
5. The child (or children) that goes over the mountain successfully is the winner.

Word Train

purpose: to identify vocabulary words
materials: classroom chairs and word cards
procedure:
1. The chairs are lined up to resemble a train.
2. Each child takes a seat (in any order).
3. The teacher displays a word card to a child. If the child answers correctly (identifies the word), he or she moves to the front of the train (engine) with chair.
4. If the child answers incorrectly, he or she remains in place and waits for another turn.
5. The next child is shown a word card. If the child correctly identifies the word, he or she moves to the front of the train and becomes the engine.
6. As the game continues, the train moves around the room.
7. The game should continue until every child has had a chance to be the engine.

Bee Careful!

purpose: to identify vocabulary words
materials: oaktag honey jars, paper clips, construction paper bees (with vocabulary words written on them) and a decorated box
procedure:
1. The teacher displays the jars and bees on a bulletin board.

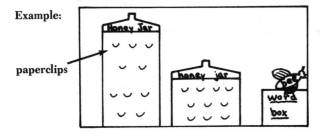

Example:

paperclips

2. The child chooses a bee from the box, says the word and if correct, places the bee on the correct honey jar. If the word begins with a capital letter (e.g., *Jim*), it is placed on the large *Honey Jar*. If the word begins with a lower-case letter, then it is placed on the small *honey jar*.

3. The child continues placing bees on the jars until he or she misses.

4. The object: Can you place all the bees on the correct jars? *BEE CAREFUL!*

5. Each child in the group should be given a turn.

Pick an Orange

purpose: to identify vocabulary words
materials: construction paper, scissors, stapler, Magic Marker and paper clips
procedure:
1. The teacher makes a bulletin board display depicting an orange tree. The teacher also makes oranges with vocabulary words written on them.

Example:

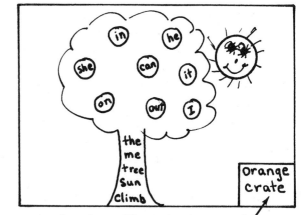

construction paper pocket, also used for storing orange words

2. The oranges are held onto the tree by paper clips.

3. The first child must climb up the tree, successfully reading the words on the way up, and then pick as many orange-words as possible.

4. The child must read the words and put them in the orange crate. The teacher then puts up more words and the next child gets a turn, etc.

Flash Card Game

purpose: to identify vocabulary words

materials: word cards
procedure:
1. A group of children stand in a line.
2. The teacher holds up a flash card.
3. The child who correctly identifies the word moves forward a certain number of steps (as indicated on the back of the word card).
4. The first child to reach a designated area is the winner.

variations:
1. The teacher holds up the word card.
2. If the child can identify the word, the teacher then reads a direction on the back of the card that tells the child to do something (e.g., *jump 3 times; sing a short song; turn around,* etc).
3. The teacher then continues onto the next child.

Candlestick Game

purpose: to identify vocabulary words
materials: construction paper and word cards
procedure:
1. The teacher makes a candlestick from construction paper.

   Example:

   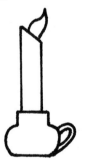

2. The word cards are placed on the floor in a straight line. The candlestick is placed at the head of the line.
3. Each participating child must say the word, then jump over it, etc. The child continues until he or she jumps over the candlestick.
4. If the child misses a word, he or she sits back down and waits for another turn.

Spider Game

purpose: to identify vocabulary words

materials: oaktag paper, construction paper spiders (with words written on them) and a decorated box.

procedure:

1. The teacher draws a large spider web on the oaktag and places the game board on the floor.

    Example:

decorated box

2. A child takes a spider from the box and says the word.
3. If the child is correct, he or she places the spider anywhere on the web and continues to choose spiders and identify the words.
4. If the child misses the word, he or she loses the turn.
5. Each child gets a turn.
6. The spiders are stored in the decorated box.

Mail-a-Word

purpose: to be able to classify known words

materials: oaktag paper, construction paper, scissors, paste, Magic Marker, word cards and a decorated box

procedure:

1. The teacher makes a large post office from the oaktag paper. Four pockets are pasted on the front of the post office, and each is labeled to designate a different category.
2. The mail (word cards) is stored in the decorated box.
3. As each child takes a card, he or she must say the word and post it in the correct pocket.
4. The word cards can be self-checked by noting the correct category on the back of the card.

Example:

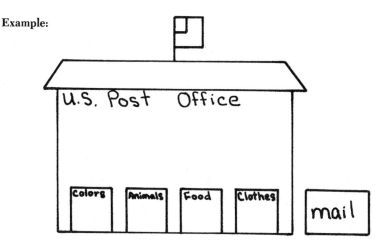

A Nutty Game

purpose: to identify vocabulary words
materials: poster board and construction paper
procedure:
1.   The teacher makes a large tree, 2 large squirrels and nuts with review words written on them.

Example:

2.   The teacher tells the children that the squirrels are hungry and they love to eat nuts.
3.   The first child takes a nut from the pocket, says the word and if correct, places the nut somewhere inside the squirrel (to symbolize that the squirrel ate it).

4. The child continues this procedure until he or she misses.

5. Each child should be given a turn.

6. If a child misses he or she waits for another turn.

variation: for a team activity, have each squirrel represent 1 team. The team whose squirrel "eats" the most is the winner.

Remove the Germ

purpose: to identify vocabulary words
materials: oaktag paper, adding machine tape, construction paper, scissors and Magic Marker
procedure:
1. The teacher makes a large body from oaktag and cuts 2 slits in the body (at the mouth and the stomach).

Example:

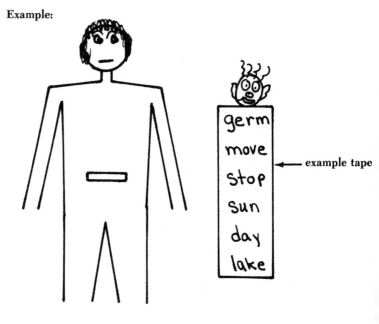

← example tape

2. The germ is made from adding machine tape. Vocabulary words are written on the tape, and the tape is threaded into the stomach slit and out of the mouth. The end of the tape that comes from the mouth first should be in the shape of a germ head.

3. Each child gets a chance to remove the germ from the body by pulling the germ from the mouth. As the words appear the child must identify them. If the child is correct, he or she pulls the germ until

another word appears, etc. If the child is incorrect, the next child gets a turn, etc.

Ride the Bus

purpose: to identify vocabulary words
materials: shoebox (painted yellow) and construction paper boys and girls (with words written on them)
procedure:
1. The teacher decorates the yellow shoebox to resemble a school bus.

   Example:
   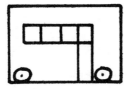

2. The teacher tells the children, "Before a child can ride the bus, he or she must read a word."
3. Each child gets a chance to read the words. If the child is correct the boy or girl shape is placed in the bus. If the child is incorrect, he or she waits for another chance.
4. The boy and girl word cards can be stored in the shoebox bus.

Wheel of Chance

purpose: to identify vocabulary words
materials: chalkboard, chalk and numbered spinner
procedure:
1. The teacher writes vocabulary words on the board and numbers each word.
2. Each child gets a chance. The child spins the spinner, notes the number referred to by the spinner and pronounces the correspondingly numbered word on the board.
3. If a child misses, he or she loses the turn. If a child is correct, he or she continues to spin the spinner, etc.

Zip-a-Word

purpose: to identify vocabulary words
materials: oaktag paper, 2 zippers, stapler and Magic Marker
procedure:
1. The teacher makes a large zip-a-word game board from the oaktag

paper. Two slits are cut in the game board just wide enough for the teeth of the zipper to show through the slit. The zipper is stapled onto the board from the back. Words are written on the front side of the game board at both sides of the zipper and positioned at different intervals.

Example:

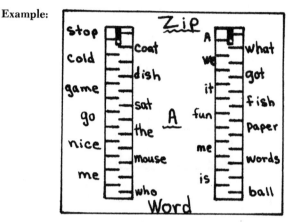

2.   Each child gets a turn to move the zippers up and down, stopping at each word and pronouncing it.

3.   This is a fun way to "zip" through vocabulary drill.

Vocabulary Number Match

purpose: to review vocabulary words and use the words in sentences
materials: word cards and dice
procedure:

1.   A number (from 2 to 12) is written in the upper right-hand corner of each vocabulary word card.

Example:

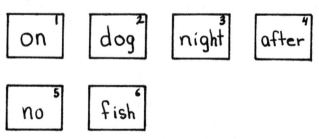

2.   Each player is given 6 or 7 word cards.

3.   In turn, each child tosses the dice and tries to match the results with 1 of the numbers on his or her word card.

4. If the child makes a match, he or she pronounces the word and uses it in a sentence. If the child is correct, the card is turned face down. If the child is incorrect, the card is left face up and the game continues.

5. The first child to turn all of his or her cards face down is the winner.

What Did I Begin With?

purpose: to identify vocabulary words, their beginning sounds and use the words in a story

materials: chalkboard and chalk

procedure:

1. The teacher writes several vocabulary words and related consonant sounds on the board.

2. A child points to 1 of the vocabulary words.

3. The child then calls on another child to say the word and pick out which one of the consonants the word begins with.

variation: a child makes up a story (orally) using as many words as possible from the vocabulary list. The child points to each word as it is used.

Word Race

purpose: to identify vocabulary words

materials: chalk, cardboard figures and word cards

Example:

procedure:

1. The teacher draws a chalk line on the floor to represent the starting line. A second line is drawn parallel to the first line to represent the goal line. Shorter lines are drawn between the start and goal lines to represent spaces for the children to land on.

2. Each player is given a cardboard figure to represent him or herself. The figure may be numbered or named by the player.

3. The players place their figures on the starting line.

4. The teacher holds up a flash card.

5. If the first child can read the card correctly, he is permitted to advance his figure 1 space.

6. The child whose figure first crosses the goal line is the winner.

    Example:

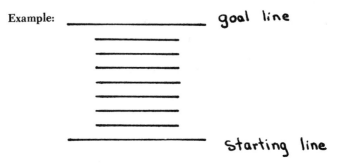

Freight Train

purpose: to identify sight words
materials: painted shoeboxes, construction paper and word cards
procedure:
1. The teacher makes several cardboard train cars. Each car should have 2 construction paper pockets glued to the sides.

    Example:

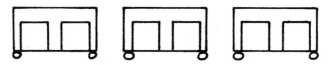

2. The teacher holds up a word card and if the player can read it, he or she may place the card in his or her train car.
3. The player whose train car has the most words (freight) at the end of the game is the winner.

Around the Circle

purpose: to identify sight words
materials: vocabulary word cards
procedure:
1. The children sit either in rows or in a circle.
2. One child starts by standing behind another child.
3. The teacher shows a word card to those 2 children.
4. The first child to say the word correctly moves on to the next child.
5. If the seated child misses, he or she remains seated. If the standing

child misses, he or she takes the place of the seated child and the other child now gets a chance to go around the circle.

6. The winner is the first child to make it around the circle successfully without being beaten.

Finders-Keepers

purpose: to identify sight words

materials: several oaktag cards marked off into 25 square blocks and word cards

Example:

There is a printed word in each box—each board is different.

procedure:

1. Each child gets a different finders-keepers game board.

2. The teacher shows a word card to the players.

3. The child who has that word on his card raises his hand, pronounces the word, points to it on his card and, if correct, is given the word card. The word card is placed on the finders-keepers game board.

4. The first child who has 5 words covered in any direction is the winner.

Get a Point

purpose: to identify sight words

materials: word list to be reviewed

procedure:

1. At the end of the day the teacher hands the children a list of vocabulary words to be reviewed.

2. The childrens' homework assignment is to search through newspapers, books and magazines for sentences containing their words.

3. The next day, each sentence brought to class earns a point for that youngster.

4. It is fun to see which child can obtain the most points.

Can You Get to the Moon?

purpose: to identify sight words
materials: oaktag game board, construction paper rockets (with words written on them) and construction paper
procedure:

1. The teacher makes a large game board. Slits are made in the game •board to insert rocket word cards.

> **Example:**

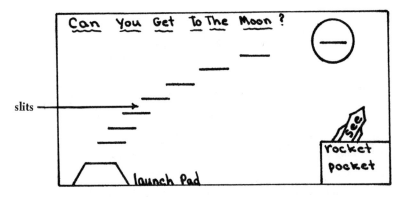

2. This is a good game for 1 child to work independently.

3. The child takes a rocket from the pocket, pronounces the word on the rocket and if correct, inserts the rocket into the first slit (launching pad). The teacher or an aid should be handy for checking.

4. The child then takes another rocket and continues in the same fashion.

5. The object is to fill in the game board and to land on the moon.

Limbo

purpose: to identify sight words
materials: word cards and broomstick
procedure:

1. Two children hold the broomstick, 1 at each end.

2. The other children form a line.

3. The teacher holds up a word card to the first child in line.
4. If the child says the word correctly, he or she gets to strut underneath the "limbo" stick.
5. If the child is incorrect, he or she goes to the end of the line.
6. The same procedure is followed for the other children.

Anyone for Ice Cream?

purpose: to identify sight words and/or phrases
materials: chalkboard and chalk
procedure:
1. The teacher draws a scene consisting of hills and an ice cream parlor on the chalkboard.

   Example:

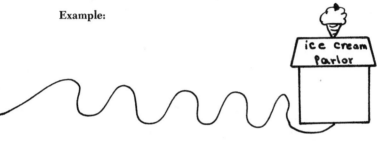

2. The teacher writes inside the hills.

   Example:

Stop first blue look bed

3. Each child gets a turn at climbing the hills.
4. When a child has climbed all the hills successfully (by saying the words correctly), his or her name is written in the ice cream parlor.
5. If there is an incorrect response, the child loses the turn and may try again later.

Colored Balls

purpose: to identify sight words and be able to recognize colors
materials: oaktag paper, Magic Marker, casette tape recorder and casette, envelope and word cards (with a word and a number written on each card)

procedure:

1. The teacher makes several game cards. Each card consists of a series of different colored balls (on the front) and an envelope (glued to the back); 9 word cards are inserted into the envelope.

   Example:

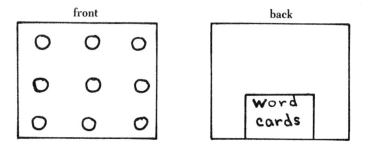

front　　　　　　　　　　　　　　　　　　back

2. The child receives a game card, inserts the casette into the tape recorder and follows directions.

3. The directions on the tape instruct the child to pick up a certain word and place it on a particular color. For example, "Pick up the word *me* and place it on the red ball." This same procedure is followed until all the word cards have been used.

4. Each word has a number beside it making checking easy. For example, the child is told "The word with the number *1* should be on the red ball, and the word is *me*."

5. The tape assists the child in self-checking his or her work.

Word Checkers

purpose:　to identify sight words
materials:　checkerboard and bottle cap markers
procedure:

1. The teacher fills in the light-colored checkerboard spaces with words. A different word is printed in each box, and each word is printed twice (once in the upper left hand corner and upside down in the lower right corner).

2. Bottle caps are used as checkers.

3. Before a child can move his checker into a space, he must be able to read the word in the space.

4. In the case of a jump, the child must be able to read both the word in the jumped over space and in the space on which he or she lands.

Let's Communicate

purpose: to be able to read words related to the communications media

materials: bulletin board, construction paper, Magic Markers, pins and word cards

procedure:

1. The teacher displays a construction paper TV, radio, newspaper and magazine on the bulletin board.

Example:

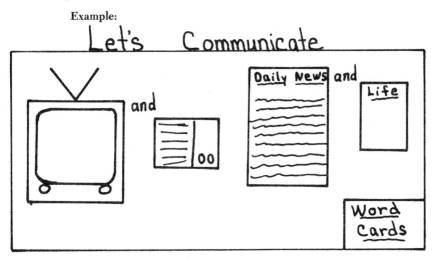

2. The child takes a word card out of the pocket (e.g., *Hee-Haw*). If the word is read correctly, he or she pins the word card near the correct media.

Example:

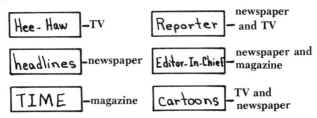

3. The game continues until all the word cards have been placed properly.

4. If a child cannot read a word, he or she goes to another word.

5. Children can keep track of how many words they could pin on.

Suckers

purpose: to identify color words
materials: construction paper, straws, scissors, glue, Magic Marker and
large jar
procedure:
1. The teacher makes several different-colored circles of the same size.
2. Two circles of the same color are glued together with a straw between
them, as in the shape of a sucker.

Example: front   back

3. The teacher makes several of these "suckers" and writes color words
on the fronts and backs of each.
4. The suckers are kept in a large jar.
5. The first child pulls out a sucker and if he can read it he gets to keep it
(on his side of the table).
6. If a child cannot read a sucker, the sucker is replaced in the jar.
7. The child that retains the most suckers is the winner.

Color Game

purpose: to identify color words
materials: paper plates, clothespins and word cards
procedure:
1. Each child receives a different-colored word-wheel and 6 clothes-
pins.
2. The teacher flashes a color word card.
3. If a child has that word on his wheel, he raises his hand and identifies
the word. If the child is correct, he clips a clothespin on to the
corresponding word on his wheel. If the child's response is incorrect
he loses the turn.
4. The first child to have clipped every color word on his wheel is the
winner.

Example:

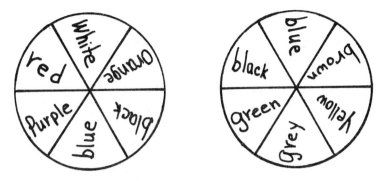

variations:

1. Each child receives a color wheel. (The various sections of the wheel are actually colored.)

2. The teacher flashes a color word card or says a color word.

3. Each child then clips a clothespin to the correct color and holds the plate up for checking.

4. This activity can be expanded to include shades (lime, violet, navy blue, etc.).

Feed the Dog

purpose: to identify sight words
materials: an oatmeal box, construction paper and Magic Marker
procedure:

1. A dog is made out of the oatmeal box and is decorated to look like a dog. A slit is made where the mouth is. Also, bones are made from construction paper with vocabulary words written on them.

   Example:

2. The child takes the bones, reads the words (1 at a time) and feeds the dog by sliding the correctly read cards through the mouth. The child continues until he or she misses.

3. The bones are stored in the dog.

4. This activity may be done independently or by a group.

Carton Capers

purpose: to identify sight words
materials: large cottage cheese cartons and small balls (with a word written on each ball)
procedure:
1. Several cottage cheese cartons are stapled together and placed on the floor.

   Example:

   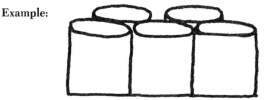

2. The children are formed into 2 teams.
3. The first team forms a line several feet away from the cartons.
4. The teacher hands each child a ball as the child receives his turn.
5. The child must read the word on the ball correctly. If he is able to do so, he gets to toss the ball toward the cartons in an attempt to land therein. If the child cannot read the word, he loses his turn.
6. When each child of the first team has had a turn, the children count the number of balls in the cartons.
7. A scorekeeper records that number on the board.
8. The second team then gets a chance to read the words and toss the balls.
9. The team with the best score is the winner.

Seasonal and Holiday Words

purpose: to identify vocabulary words
materials: construction paper, word cards, envelopes and paper clips
procedure:
1. The teacher makes several season-related objects and related word cards from construction paper.
2. The season could be Autumn, Halloween, Thanksgiving, Christmas, Winter, Valentine's Day, Spring, Easter, Summer, etc.
3. An envelope containing the related words is glued on the back of each large object.
4. The child takes the words out of the envelope and, if said correctly, gets to pin the words on the seasonal object.

Example:

paperclips

Headlines

purpose: to define unfamiliar words
materials: newspapers, dictionaries, paper and pencil
procedure:
1. The teacher chooses several newspaper headlines and displays them on the chalk ledge.
2. The students are to rewrite the headlines in their own words using a dictionary to find the meanings of unfamiliar words.
3. Each student reads and shares his or her headlines with the others in the group.

Vocabulary Enrichment

purpose: to identify objects by groups
materials: dictionary, pencil and paper
procedure:
1. The teacher enriches a child's vocabulary by introducing and discussing terms used to identify groups of objects. (e.g., a *flock* of sheep; a *swarm* of bees).
2. The children then are provided a worksheet containing a number of terms. Using a dictionary they are to complete the phrases in which the terms appear.

> **Example:**   A string of _____ .
>
> A set of _____ .
>
> A cluster of _____ .
>
> A tribe of _____ .
>
> A crowd of _____ .

A bunch of _____ .

A gaggle of _____ .

A school of _____ .

A pack of _____ .

A grove of _____ .

A litter of _____ .

A fleet of _____ .

A squad of _____ .

A stock of _____ .

A herd of _____ .

A pride of _____ .

11 structural analysis: the basics of word forms and variations

Structural analysis is the study of plurals, prefixes and suffixes, syllabification, compound words, contractions, and homonyms-antonyms-synonyms. In this chapter, each of these subjects is supplemented by numerous activities and games, all designed to ensure proper concept introduction and exposure. In addition, each subject area contains a worksheet for follow-up reinforcement.

The skills covered include word construction, analysis of word forms, identification of and distinguishing words, root words and components and the relationship of a part of a word to its whole.

PLURALS

Plural Concentration

purpose: to match identical plural words
materials: oaktag game board, construction paper and word cards (duplicate sets)
procedure:
1. The game board is divided into 20 sections with a construction paper pocket in each section.

2. The teacher places a word card (plural forms) in each pocket; 2 sets of 10 cards should be used so that there will be 10 matches each time the game board is set up.

3. The game is played like "Concentration." Each child takes a turn by removing a card from a pocket, reading the word, guessing where the matching card is and removing the matching word from its pocket, if correct. If the child matches plural words, 1 point is scored. The child continues to score points so long as matches are made.

4. The word cards are stored in the game board pockets.

   Example:

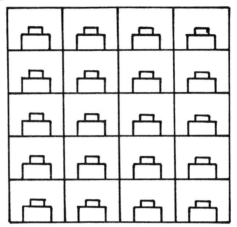

variation: match a word card with a picture card.

   Example:

Carrot Patch

purpose: to match plural ending with words
materials: bulletin board, construction paper, scissors and pins
procedure:

1. The teacher makes a carrot patch display.

2. The carrots contain the singular form of the word, and in the farmer's basket are cards containing the various forms of plural endings (e.g., *s, es, ies, ves*).

3. The child takes a card from the farmer's basket and matches the plural form to the correct singular form appearing on the carrot.

4. The plural card is pinned to the carrot.

Example:

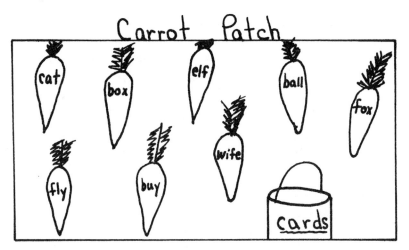

Fill the Squares

purpose: to identify and distinguish between singular and plural word forms

materials: manila paper, crayons and word cards (containing plural words and singular words)

procedure:

1. Each child is given a piece of manila paper at least 12″ square.

2. The child folds the paper twice in each direction (i.e., right to left, and top to bottom) to form 16 squares.

3. The child is instructed to color in alternate squares lightly or any other pattern he or she chooses to create.

   Example:

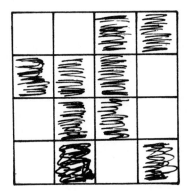

4. The teacher instructs the group to look carefully as he or she displays word cards.

5. If a child can identify the word, he raises his hand. The teacher may ask a child who has raised his hand to identify the word, and if the child is correct he receives the card and places it on his board.

6. All singular words are placed on the white squares.

7. All plural words are placed on the colored squares.

8. The game continues until all the word cards are given out.

9. This is a fun activity to see the different patterns the children have made.

Tomato Patch

purpose: to match and identify plurals

materials: oaktag paper, construction paper, Magic Marker, paste, envelope and paper clips

procedure:

1. The teacher makes a large game board from oaktag. Many tomatoes are made from construction paper and pasted on the board (each labeled with a word in its singular form). Also many green leaves are made with the plural form of the tomato words written on them. The leaves are stored in an envelope pasted on the back of the game board.

   Example:

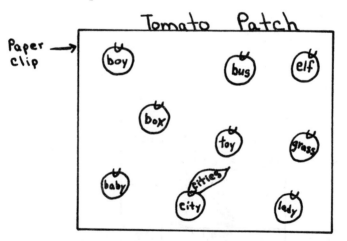

2. The children are to match the correct leaf (plural form) with the correct tomato (singular form).

3. This activity can be made self-checking by writing the answer on the back of each leaf.

Example: front   back

Singular and Plural Match

purpose: to match singular and plural words and pictures
materials: word cards and a large chart with several pictures, showing objects in singular form and in pairs or groups (See page 180.)
procedure:
1. The child is given word cards containing the singular and plural form of each object on the chart.
2. The child chooses the word that goes with each picture.
3. The words can be fastened to the chart with a paper clip.

PREFIXES AND SUFFIXES

Prefix Match

purpose: to identify root words and prefixes
materials: oaktag paper, word cards (containing root words and prefixes) and Magic Marker
procedure:
1. The teacher makes 3 large apples from oaktag and divides each apple into 2 parts (prefix and root word).

Example:

The group is divided into 3 teams.

2. The teacher prepares a deck of cards containing root words and prefixes.

Worksheet

Directions: Cut out the word "plural" and paste
it in the correct picture box.

Cut and paste

Plural

Plural

Plural

Plural

Plural

3. Each player is dealt a certain number of cards.

4. Each player on each team draws a card from his or her pile. (Each team is playing at the same time.) The team members may share the cards they draw and attempt to match their cards to form a word. If a match is made, the word is placed on their team apple.

   Example:

5. If a match cannot be made, the cards are discarded.

6. The game continues with each team continuing to draw, share, match and discard.

7. The team making the most matches with their cards is the winner.

Prefix Problem

purpose: to identify prefixes
materials: pocket chart, prefix cards and sentence strips
procedure:

1. The teacher prepares several sentence strips with the prefixes left out.

   Example:

   > Will you _____ turn by eight?

2. The sentence strips and prefix cards are placed in the pocket chart.

   Example:

   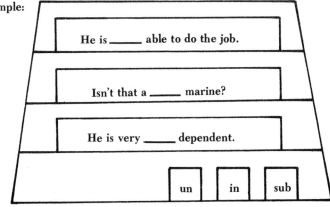

3. Each child in the group gets a turn at reading a sentence, choosing the correct prefix and inserting it into the sentence strip.

4. The teacher may put new sentence strips in the chart and the game continues.

Drum-Up New Words

purpose: to identify suffixes and be able to make new words
materials: oaktag drums (containing suffixes), word cards, paper, pencil and decorated box
procedure:
1. The teacher makes oaktag drums and displays them on the chalk ledge.

   Example:

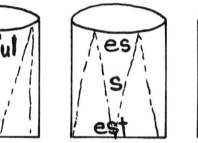

2. Each child draws a word card from the box and tries to make as many new words as possible by using the suffixes on the drums.

3. Each child's new word forms are written on paper.

   Example: farm ⟶ farmer, farming
   happy ⟶ happiness, happily, happier

4. At the end of the activity, each child gets a chance to share his or her words.

Suffix Scene

purpose: to identify suffixes, make new words and use the new words in a sentence
materials: chalkboard and chalk
procedure:
1. the teacher writes several suffixes and words on the chalkboard.

Example: <u>ing</u>, <u>ed</u>, <u>ly</u>, <u>ment</u>, <u>est</u>, <u>er</u>, <u>ed</u>, <u>mess</u>, <u>ful</u>

health	small	run
paint	ship	walk
cool	quick	happy
please	fast	place

2. Each child orally chooses a word and a suffix, pronounces his or her new word and uses it in a sentence.

variation: each child can use the root word in a sentence first and then use the new word in a sentence.

Dial-a-Suffix

purpose: to identify suffixes and make new words
materials: a cardboard disc with words written near the outside edge and center mounted hands containing various suffixes

Example:

procedure:
1. The teacher makes several of these discs.
2. The child dials the hands and matches the correct ending with a root word.
3. For self-checking, the root words and their endings can be indicated on the back of the disc.
4. This is a good activity for independent work.

A Suffix-Prefix Game

purpose: to identify prefixes and suffixes and make new words
materials: 3 sets of word cards

procedure:

1. The teacher writes prefixes on the first set of word cards, root words on the second, and suffixes on the third set. Each set is color-coded so they can be quickly grouped.

2. The cards are placed in 3 piles.

3. The child sorts through the piles and arranges the cards to form as many words as possible.

4. Have the child list the words he or she has found.

Pull-a-Word

purpose: to use prefixes and suffixes and make new words

materials: oaktag cards (with parallel slits, and a word written on each card), oaktag strips (containing prefixes and suffixes) and a decorated box

Example:

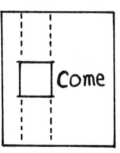 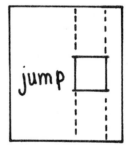

procedure:

1. The child takes the cards and strips (stored in the decorated box) and attempts to match the correct strip with the correct card to make a new word(s).

Example:

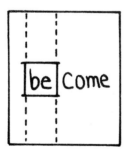 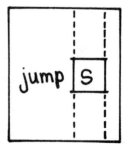

2. The child can take the completed cards to the teacher, an aid or an older student for checking.

Reading Pole

purpose: to identify prefixes and suffixes
materials: broomstick or curtain rod, metal rings, white oaktag squares (for root words), green oaktag squares (for prefixes), red oaktag squares (for suffixes), or any other color combination, and worksheet (See page 186.)
procedure:
1. The teacher punches holes in each oaktag square and puts all the prefix cards on 1 metal ring, all root words on a second metal ring, and all suffix cards on a third metal ring. The broomstick or curtain rod then is inserted through the rings.

   Example:

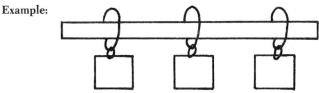

2. The child flips through the cards and sets up correct combinations.

   Example:

3. A child may use this as an independent activity for review of root words, prefixes and suffixes.

SYLLABLES

Ride a Camel

purpose: to identify the correct number of syllables in a word
materials: oaktag, word cards (people-shaped) and a bulletin board
procedure:
1. The teacher displays camels on a bulletin board.

Worksheet

Directions: Underline the <u>prefix</u> once and the
<u><u>suffix</u></u> twice in each sentence.

1. Please return the books.

2. The farmer is unable to do the milking.

3. A submarine goes below the water.

4. The flowers are colorful.

5. Good health habits prevent sickness.

6. The children are sleepy.

7. The child was yelling and shouting.

8. The man had to repaint the fence.

Example:

2. The child takes a word-person from the pocket (e.g.,) and decides which camel the person can ride. If the word is a 1-syllable word, the person is attached (paper-clipped) to the camel with 1 hump. If the word is a 2-syllable word (e.g.,) then the person rides the camel with 2 humps, etc.

3. The game continues until all the people are riding camels.

4. This activity can be made self-checking by indicating the correct number of syllables on the back of each word-person.

Here's the Scoop!

purpose: to identify the correct number of syllables in words

materials: a large piece of oaktag, construction paper ice cream scoops of various colors, construction paper ice cream cones (with words written on them), a construction paper pocket and paper clips

Example:

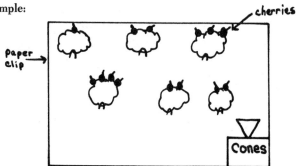

procedure:

1. The child takes the cones out of the pocket and says the word. As the child says the word, he or she listens for its number of parts (syllables).

Example:

2. The child then decides how many syllables the word has and hooks the cone to the correct ice cream scoop, which displays the same number of cherries (symbolizing syllables heard).

Example:

3. When all the cones have been placed on the game board, the child can self-check his or her results by checking the number of cherries on the back of each cone.

Example:

Syllable Game

purpose: to identify the correct number of syllables in words

materials: poster board, scissors, pins, Magic Marker, picture cards, clear contact paper and a decorated box

procedure:

1. The teacher makes a game board from poster board and covers it with contact paper.

Example:

Number of Syllables			
1	2	3	4

2. The pictures are taken from the storage box. Each picture is examined and the child decides how many syllables the pictured object has.

3. The child places the picture in the column representing the number of syllables identified.

4. When the game board is filled, the child can self-check by turning over the picture card and checking the number of syllables indicated.

TV Fun

purpose: to identify words and their number of syllables
materials: an old TV set (or one made from a box), mural paper and crayons
procedure:

1. The teacher writes a variety of words on sectioned-off mural paper.

2. The children are instructed to draw the number of pictures to coincide with the number of syllables in each section.

Example:

3. When the mural is completed the group presents their display to the other children in the class.

4. The mural is displayed through the TV set.

Example:

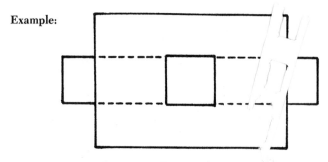

Two children slide the mural across the screen.

Ride the Number Train

purpose: to identify the number of syllables a word contains
materials: bulletin board, construction paper and word cards
procedure:
  1.   The teacher makes a bulletin board display showing a train.

Example:

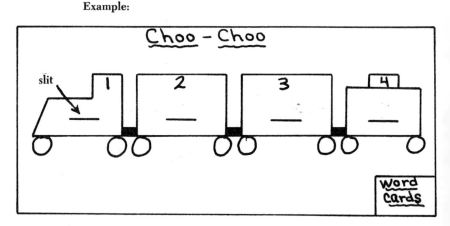

  2.   The pocket contains words of 1, 2, 3, and 4 syllables.
  3.   The child draws a word from the pocket and places it on the correct numbered train car corresponding to the number of syllables the word contains. (The word card is inserted into the slit in the train car.)
  4.   The game continues until all the cards are dispersed correctly and the child indicates that he or she can ride the number train.
  5.   This activity can be made self-checking by indicating the number of syllables on the back of each word card.

Dot, Dot-Dot, or Dot-Dot-Dot

purpose: to identify the number of syllables a word contains
materials: word cards and several oaktag squares with 1, 2 or 3 dots

   Example:

procedure:
   1.   Each child is given several dotted cards.
   2.   The teacher holds up a word card.
   3.   Each child must decide on the number of syllables that the word contains and hold up a corresponding dot card.

   Example:

A Cupful of Syllables

purpose: to identify words, pictures and their number of syllables
materials: construction paper cups, magazines, scissors, paste and worksheet (See page 192.)
procedure:
   1.   The teacher displays the cups in the room. Each cup designates a certain number of syllables.

   Example:

Worksheet

Directions: Write the number of syllables each
box contains. Color the pictures.

apples

tiger

television

tree

flowers

sunshine

crocodile

rabbit

ice cream cones

envelope

2. The children are given magazines, scissors and paste.

3. The children are to cut out words and pictures, decide on the correct number of syllables each word or picture contains and paste the words and pictures on the corresponding cup.

4. This activity continues until there is a cupful of syllables.

COMPOUND WORDS

Compound Bank

purpose: to identify compound words
materials: chart paper, word cards, paper clips and envelope
procedure:

1. The teacher writes several sentences on chart paper. The teacher includes only a part of the compound word in the sentence.

     Example:

> The fire_____ put the fire out.

2. In turn, each child reads a sentence and chooses the correct word from the compound bank to complete the sentence. The word card is placed on the line and secured with a paper clip.

     Example:

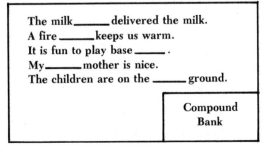

> The milk_____ delivered the milk.
> A fire _____ keeps us warm.
> It is fun to play base _____ .
> My_____ mother is nice.
> The children are on the _____ ground.
>
> Compound
> Bank

Word Mixture

purpose: to identify compound words
materials: bulletin board, construction paper, paper bags, word cards and a pocket chart
procedure:

1. The teacher makes a bulletin board display to reinforce compound words.

   Example:

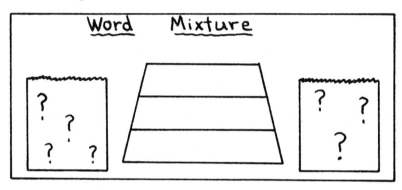

2. The word cards are placed in the paper bags.
3. The child is to take a word card from each bag and continue until he or she has made a match (compound word).
4. The newly formed word then is placed in the pocket chart.
5. When the activity is completed, the teacher or an aid can check for correctness.

Compound It

purpose: to be able to make compound words from given words
materials: paper and pencil
procedure:

1. The children are divided into 2 teams.
2. The teacher says a word. (The teacher should use words to which another word can be added to make a compound word.)

   Example: *snow*

3. All the children write *snow* on their paper.
4. By adding other words, the children make as many compound words as they can.

Example: *snowball*
            snowflake
            snowman
            snowplow

5. The teacher calls "time" and the team that has the most "snow" words—scoring 1 point for each different snow word—is the winner of the round.

variation: the teacher may want to give an extra point for words spelled correctly.

Compound Words Throughout the Year

purpose: to identify compound words
materials: oaktag paper, Magic Marker, paper and pencil
procedure:
1. The teacher makes a large oaktag display of compound word pictures depicting happenings throughout the year.

Example:

2. Each child is to write the number and the compound word associated with the picture on his or her paper correctly and neatly.
3. The paper may be handed into the teacher for checking.
4. In addition, the child may want to draw and color the picture that goes with his or her written compound words.

Compound Match

purpose: to be able to build compound words
materials: several word cards and blank cards

procedure:

1. The word cards and blank cards (wild cards) are shuffled, and each player receives 5. The remaining cards are placed face down in the center.

2. The first player draws a card from the pile and tries to make a compound match. If the child is able to do so, he places the two matching cards face up in front of him for all to see.

    Example: | Sun | | Shine |

3. If the player cannot make a match, he must discard 1 card.

4. The next player, always to the left of the last player, may use the discarded card to make a match or may draw from the pile. The same procedure is followed for all the players.

5. The game continues until each player has made as many matches as possible.

6. The player with the most matches is the winner.

Egg Match

purpose: to identify compound words

materials: flannel board, flannel tape, oaktag paper, scissors, Magic Marker, and worksheet (See page 197.)

procedure:

1. The teacher should have a flannel board available for this egg-match activity.

2. Several oaktag egg halves (with flannel tape on the backs) are dispersed on the flannel board.

    Example:

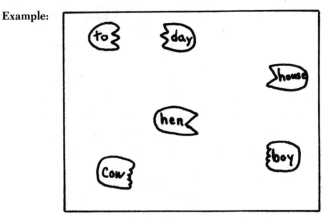

Worksheet

Directions: Write the compound word the pictures represent.

Example:

raindrop

3. The child looks carefully at all the egg halves and tries to match all the compound words successfully.

4. When the child has completed the activity, the teacher or an aid can check for accuracy.

CONTRACTIONS

Short-Cut Words

purpose: to introduce the concept of contractions
materials: chalkboard and chalk
procedure:
  1. The teacher produces the following display on the board:

2. The teacher tells the children the following story:

> There once was a man who had a field where he grew corn. During the summer no one was allowed to cross the field. So, people had to go the long way around.

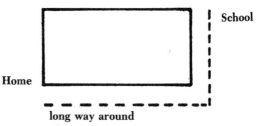

But, in the winter, snow covered the frozen ground and people were able to take a short cut.

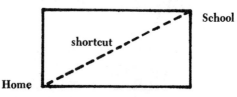

3. The same story is applied to contractions:

Sometimes we use the long way around, and sometimes we use the short cut way to say or write the same thought.

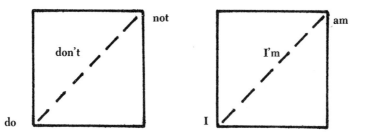

Reveal the Contraction

purpose: to identify the contraction

materials: sentence strips, oaktag paper squares (with contractions written on them), construction paper and paper clips

procedure:

1. The teacher writes several sentences on strips and displays them on a bulletin board. A contraction pocket is made from construction paper, and the contraction word cards are stored in the pocket.

Example:

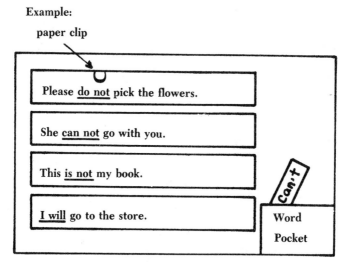

2. The child selects the correct contraction card from the pocket and hooks it (paper clips it) over the correct words in each sentence.

3. When all contraction words have been placed on the sentences, the child checks his or her work by turning over the contraction word card where the contraction components are indicated.

Contraction Match

purpose: to be able to identify contractions

materials: overhead projector, transparency, grease pencil and worksheet (See below.)

procedure:

1. The teacher prepares several contraction match exercises on a transparency for the overhead projector.
2. The children gather by the projector and watch as the teacher flashes the activity on the screen (or the activity can be projected on the blackboard).

Worksheet			
do not	haven't	did not	wasn't
have not	isn't	was not	didn't
is not	don't	should not	shouldn't
could not	you're	I will	I'll
I am	couldn't	you will	he's
you are	I'm	he is	you'll
she will	they'll	will not	I've
she is	she'll	we will	won't
they will	she's	I have	we'll

3. The child is to read the word, find its contraction and match the words and contractions by drawing lines with the grease pencil. (If the activity is projected on the board, the child should use a piece of chalk to draw the lines.)

4. Each child should get a turn at matching the contractions.

Toby's Poem

purpose: to detect the advantages of contractions in poem writing
materials: a poem
procedure:

1. A poem—such as *Toby's Poem*—offers many opportunities to review and reinforce the concept of contractions.

> *Toby's Poem*
> Toby the turtle,
> that's what they call me.
> I am the turtle
> that's under the tree.
>
> Here's a short poem
> I've written for you.
> It's my way to say,
> "Hi, how do you do?"
>
> I like to make friends
> wherever I go.
> I'm sure you will be
> a fine friend to know.

2. The following are suggested ways in which to use poems:

a. Poems provide good introductions to motivate a discussion of contractions and their uses.

b. A poem may be projected on a screen or chalkboard and the children can underline the contractions.

c. The teacher can reproduce the poem on a ditto so that the children can underline the contractions and write the words that make up the contraction.

d. The teacher can use the poem as a writing lesson by having the children copy the poem and write the contraction components.

e. The teacher can encourage the children to make up and write their own poems using contractions.

f. The teacher can display the poem on chart paper with matching word cards to be matched to the contractions.

g. One child reads the poem and the other children in the group clap every time a contraction word is heard.

Oaktag Wheels

purpose: to be able to identify contractions
materials: oaktag wheels (with contractions written on them) and clothes-pins (with contraction components written on them)
procedure:
  1. The teacher makes several wheels and makes them available for the children to manipulate.

  Example:

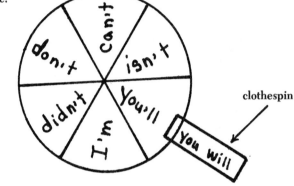

clothespin

  2. The child is to match the correct clothespin to the correct contraction on the wheel.
  3. This activity can be made self-checking by indicating the correct contraction components on the backs of the oaktag wheels.

Guess Who?

purpose: to match contractions and their components
materials: oaktag squares and worksheet (See page 203.)
procedure:
  1. The teacher writes contractions on half of the oaktag squares and the contraction components on the remaining oaktag squares.
  2. These squares then are dispersed among the students.
  3. At a signal from the teacher, the children must find their partners. When the correct partner is found, the partners sit down.

variations:
  1. The teacher may deal out contraction word cards, component word cards and sentence strips containing the contractions.
  2. At a signal from the teacher, the 3 related students must find each other and match up.

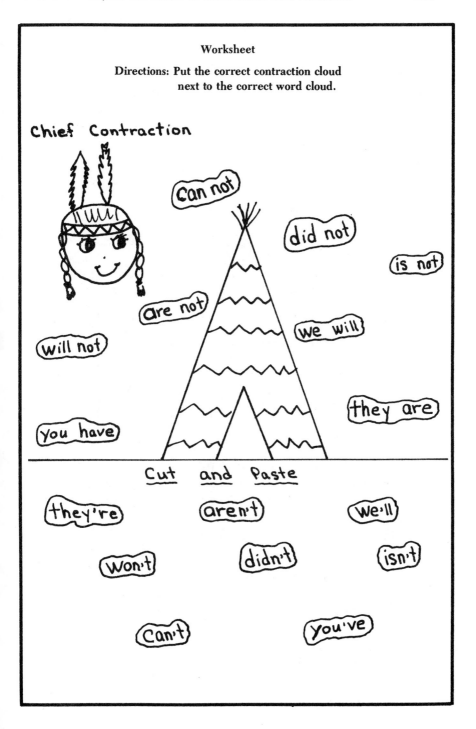

Worksheet

Directions: Put the correct contraction cloud
next to the correct word cloud.

Chief Contraction

Can not

did not

is not

are not

will not

we will

you have

they are

Cut and Paste

they're

aren't

we'll

won't

didn't

isn't

can't

you've

HOMONYMS, ANTONYMS AND SYNONYMS

Handsome Homonyms

purpose: to identify homonyms and use them correctly in a sentence

materials: construction paper, oaktag paper, scissors, pencil and a decorated box (containing construction paper hands with words written on them)

procedure:

1.   The teacher prepares a game board made from oaktag.

   Example:

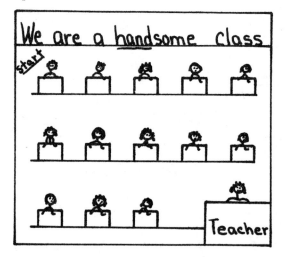

2.   Each child is given construction paper, scissors and a pencil.

3.   The child is to trace his or her hand on the construction paper and cut it out. When labeled with the child's name, it becomes the child's marker.

4.   The first child in the group draws a hand from the box.

   Example:

5.   The child must identify the word and use it in a sentence.

   Example: The sky is *blue*.

6.   The child then must say the word's homonym form and use it in a sentence.

   Example: The wind *blew*.

7. If the child identifies the word, its homonym and uses both words in sentences successfully, he or she may advance to the first desk on the game board.

8. If the child is incorrect, he or she loses the turn and the word-hand goes back into the box.

9. The game continues until someone has reached the teacher's desk on the game board. The first person to reach the teacher's desk is the winner.

Baseball

purpose: to identify synonyms, antonyms and homonyms, and use them in a sentence

materials: word cards

procedure:

1. The teacher sets up an area of the classroom to resemble a baseball diamond. (Chairs are used as bases and a mat is used for home plate.)

   Example:

   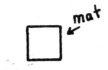

1ˢᵗ base

3ʳᵈ base

2ⁿᵈ base

2. The game is played with 2 teams.

3. The first child (batter) of the first team to bat stands on the mat and the teacher "pitches" (flashes) a word card (e.g., *hot*).

4. The batter first must identify the word, provide either the synonym, antonym or homonym form of the word and tell the teacher what form he or she gave. The child then uses the new word form in a sentence.

   Example:

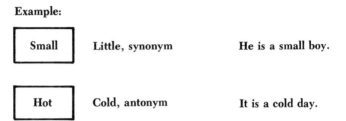

| Small | Little, synonym | He is a small boy. |
| Hot | Cold, antonym | It is a cold day. |

5. If the child successfully completes the exercise, he or she proceeds to first base.
6. The game continues with the second member of the team being the batter, etc.
7. When there are 3 misses (outs) by the first team, the opposing team tries their skill at baseball.
8. At the end of the game, the team with the most runs is the winner.

Touchdown

purpose: to identify synonyms, antonyms and homonyms
materials: oaktag paper, Magic Marker, construction paper, football shapes of different colors and word cards
procedure:
   1. The teacher makes a large game board with word cards placed on each 10-yard line.

   Example:

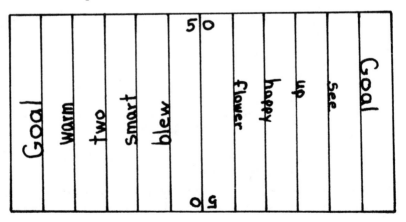

2. The different-colored football markers are kept in a construction paper pocket glued to the back of the game board.

3. The group is divided into 2 teams.

4. Each of the teams starts at the 50-yard line and progresses toward a goal.

5. Each team member, in turn, must give the yard-line word's synonym, antonym or homonym (no repeats). If the child uses a synonym or antonym, he or she first must identify the yard line word and then the synonym or antonym. If the child uses a homonym, the word must be used in a sentence.

6. If a player continues with no mistakes, he or she scores a touchdown for the team.

7. The opposing team then gets a chance to read their words.

8. If the team member makes a mistake ("fumbles"), he or she is out of the game ("benched").

9. The team that scores the most touchdowns is the winner.

10. The yard-line words can be changed and the game continues.

Synonym Showoff

purpose: to identify synonyms (words and pictures)
materials: oaktag paper, Magic Marker, magazines, scissors and paste
procedure:

1. The teacher prepares 3 displays on oaktag paper with a picture and a title on each.

   Example:

2. The children are given magazines and are told to cut out similar words and/or pictures, which are to be pasted on the correct display.

3. When the displays are completed they may be displayed for everyone to see.

Rewrite a Story

purpose: to be able to identify and correctly use antonyms in a sentence

materials: chart paper, paper and pencil

procedure:
1. The teacher prepares a chart story with certain words underlined and a word bank to be used for substituting new words for the underlined words.

   Example:

	Word Bank
The <u>little</u> girl got a new dog <u>for</u> a pet. The dog had <u>white</u> fur, four large feet and a <u>warm</u> nose. The dog and the girl went for a <u>walk</u>. It was a <u>sunny</u> day.	little big black cold run cloudy

2. The children are instructed to copy the story on paper and substitute for the underlined words, words from the word bank having the opposite meaning.
3. The teacher or an aid should check the work for accuracy.

May I?

purpose: to identify and match synonyms, antonyms and homonyms

materials: word cards

procedure:
1. This is a good game for a small group of children.
2. Each child is dealt 6 cards.
3. The object of the game is to match the cards to obtain matching antonyms, synonyms and homonyms.
4. The first player calls on another player in the group (any 1 of the players), "May I have_____?" (The child names a card in his or her hand and asks for its antonym, synonym or homonym.)

   Example: "May I have the opposite to *up*?"

5. If the player called on has the card requested, he must give it up. If he does not have the requested card, he says, "No, you may not," and the first player must wait for another turn.

6. If the first player gets the card requested, he displays his pair face up on the table and continues to request cards until he misses.

7. The player with the most pairs is the winner.

Make It Balance

purpose: to identify synonyms and antonyms
materials: oaktag paper, construction paper, Magic Markers, word cards and paper clips
procedure:
   1. The teacher makes a house and ladder display on a large piece of oaktag; a bulletin board can be used to display the scene.

   Example:

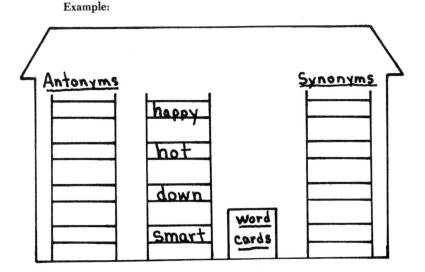

2. The synonym and antonym word cards are placed in the word pocket.

3. The child draws a card from the pocket and places it on the correct rung of the correct ladder (using paper clips to hold the word cards in place).

4. The object is to keep the ladders from falling from the house. If the ladders are balanced properly they will not topple over.

5. The word cards can be made self-checking with the correct solution indicated on the back.

Snowman Game

purpose: to identify synonyms and antonyms

materials: construction paper snowmen (with flannel backing), flannel board, blackboard and chalk

procedure:

1. The snowmen contain the words *synonym* and *antonym* and are placed on the flannel board. (Several duplicate sets should be made and displayed.)

    Example:

2. The teacher writes a word on the board (e.g., "little").

3. The first child says a sentence using the synonym or antonym form of the word written on the board.

    Example: The dog is *big*.

4. Another child must decide whether the first child used the written word's synonym or antonym form.

5. A child raises his or her hand and indicates "antonym." An acknowledgement from the teacher indicates the correctness of the response.

6. If the child is correct he or she receives an antonym snowman.

7. If the child is incorrect, he or she must wait for another turn.

8. The game continues with another word and a different child saying a sentence.

9. When all the snowmen are given out to the children, the game is over.

10. The child with the most snowmen is the winner.

Smile!

purpose: to provide practice in identifying words with opposite meanings
materials: oaktag game board (with faces drawn in and a word on each face), Magic Marker, paper clips and an envelope (containing smiles with words written on them)

Example:

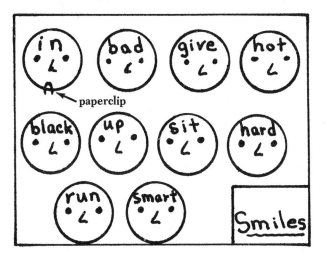

examples

procedure:
1. The child must give the faces smiles by drawing a smile word card from the pocket and placing it on the correct face that has the opposite meaning.
2. The activity can be made self-checking by indicating the correct opposite on the back of each smile.

Homonym Hop

purpose: to identify homonyms and use them correctly in sentences
materials: chalkboard, chalk and eraser
procedure:
1. The teacher writes several sentences on the board. Each sentence should contain word choices.

> **Example:** I see-sea the blue-blew sky.
>
> The flower-flour smells so sweet.
>
> The girl road-rode her bike.
>
> The bee-be stung the baby.

2. This is an active activity. The first child must "hop" up to the board, read the first sentence and decide on the correct words. The child then erases the word(s) that does not belong.

3. The teacher is present to check for accuracy.

4. If there is an incorrect erasure, the word(s) is written again and another child tries.

5. This activity continues until all the children have had an opportunity to "homonym hop."

The Pair-Pear Tree

purpose: to identify homonyms
materials: a bulletin board, construction paper and pins
procedure:

1. This can be a total class activity.

2. The teacher makes a large tree and displays it on the bulletin board.

3. The teacher makes many construction paper pears, which are stored in a pocket near the tree.

    Example:

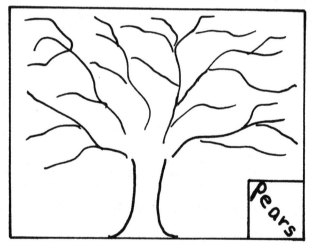

4. Any child can participate if he can write a pair of homonyms on the pears.

    Example:

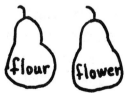

5. If a child can write a pair of homonyms, he is permitted to pin his pears on the tree (no repeats!).

6. The activity continues until the tree is covered with pears (pairs).

Crossword Puzzle

purpose: to identify and write antonyms (opposites)
materials: chalkboard and chalk
procedure:

1. The teacher makes a simple variation of a crossword puzzle on the board. The teacher also provides a list of words.

   Example:

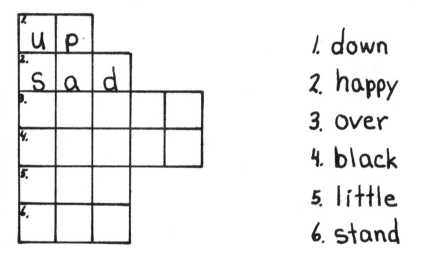

2. The child must give an opposite word for each numbered word and write it in the puzzle. The sectioned-off spaces of the crossword should indicate the number of letters the new word contains.

3. Each child in the group can do a different word.

4. When the puzzle is completed a new puzzle can be made.

Frying Pan

purpose: to identify homonyms through context clues
materials: an oral activity
procedure:

1. One child is designated "It" and leaves the room.

2. The class then decides on 2 sentences, replacing the homonym with the words *frying pan*.

> **Example:** Sue's new dress is *frying pan*.
>
> The wind *frying pan* very hard.

3. The child who is "It" returns to the room and listens as 1 of the children repeats both sentences.

4. The child must guess the homonym from the sentences, using the contexts of the sentences as clues.

Same or Different

purpose: to identify homonyms, antonyms and synonyms
materials: oaktag squares, Magic Marker, decorated box, and worksheet (See page 215.)
procedure:

1. The teacher writes 2 words on each square. The words are pairs of homonyms, antonyms and synonyms.

2. The child takes the word cards and sorts them into 3 piles, indicating to the teacher or an aid which words have the same meaning (synonym), which are opposite (antonym) and which words sound the same (homonym).

3. The teacher or an aid checks the piles for accuracy.

4. The cards may be stored in the decorated box.

Compiling a Class Book

purpose: to develop the understanding of homonyms and antonyms and to learn the relationship between spelling and meaning
materials: construction paper, manila paper, crayons and stapler
procedure:

1. The teacher makes a large homonym class bookcover and a large antonym class bookcover.

> **Example:**

Worksheet

Directions: Tell whether the following pairs of words are synonyms, antonyms or homonyms.

2. The children receive manila paper on which they draw, label and color pictures to go into the class books.

3. When the children have made many pages, the teacher then staples the pages and covers together to make a class book.

4. This activity makes a very attractive classroom project and display.

Synonym Bingo

purpose: to identify synonyms
materials: game cards (with words written in the boxes), word cards and markers

Example:

big	little	happy
cry	run	cook
talk	Dad	good

procedure:

1. Each child receives a synonym bingo board and some markers.

2. The caller will announce a word (e.g., "large"), and the players must cover up the word's synonym if they have the synonym on their cards.

3. The first person to get 3 in a row (across or up and down) is the winner.

12   activities to stimulate pupil interest and creativity

The following activities can be used during a school day (beginning, middle or end) to stimulate pupil interest, imagination and creativity. These activities can be used as teaching aids, and are useful gimmicks to help start the day, or to introduce or reinforce various concepts. In addition, they are general "fun" projects for the students.

Word-by-Word Reading

The teacher should have a proficient student tape record a passage from one of the classroom books. Later, slower or less proficient students can read the passage in conjunction with the tape recording. Thus, the student reads the material and hears each word as he or she reads it.

Crazy Days

The teacher should encourage the children to participate in special day activities. These days can be established as a once-a-month activity or on a more infrequent basis. These occasions are ideal for exposing the class to new and different experiences and to stimulate class discussion.
Several examples of crazy days are as follows:

tie day: The children wear the oddest ties they can find. At school, the students discuss and write about ties and share their stories.

hat day: The children wear old hats to school or make their own hats from scrap material, paper or even trash.

color day: The children dress in odd colors and while at school they write stories about the class dress.

Guess What I Am Doing!

The teacher may act out a number of verbs and ask the children to guess what he or she is doing. The children should respond by answering in sentence fashion. The teacher should listen for an -*ing* response.

Example:			
1.	buttoning	13.	sleeping
2.	eating	14.	winking
3.	drinking	15.	shaking
4.	smelling	16.	tasting
5.	kicking	17.	yawning
6.	crying	18.	writing
7.	clapping	19.	throwing
8.	rocking	20.	hopping
9.	sweeping	21.	scratching
10.	sneezing	22.	running
11.	pulling	23.	sitting
12.	pushing	24.	jumping

Use Your Ruler

This is a good activity either for a small group of students or the entire class. Materials required for this project are rulers, pencils and paper, such as graph paper with ½″ squares. The teacher should write the following directions on the board or provide the directions to the children on ditto paper. The finished papers may be displayed in the classroom for all to see and enjoy.

directions:

1. Draw a house 3″ high.
2. Draw a rectangle 2″ long and 1″ high.
3. Draw a man 5″ high.
4. Draw a girl 3″ high.
5. Draw a dog 2″ high.
6. Draw a line 5″ long.
7. Draw a skyscraper 7″ high.
8. Draw a car 5″ long.

Tutors

The teacher may employ a wide range of tutors to assist his or her teaching program. For example, besides the proficient students and those from higher grades (as well as aids and parents), the teacher may use tape recorders, overhead projectors, dittoes, record players, Language Masters, etc.

Moreover, if appropriate films or filmstrips are available, the teacher should not hesitate to employ such materials or to supplement such devices with his or her own instructions and directions.

Collage

After the presentation of a number of reading-related skills, and after the children have developed an adequate sight vocabulary, the teacher may have the children prepare a collage of what they have learned. The basic ingredients are chart paper, pictures, letters or words from old magazines, scissors and paste.

When the collage is finished, the children will have made a colorful, visual presentation of what they have learned. The collage can be displayed in the classroom for all the children to see or attached to a hallway bulletin board for sharing with the rest of the school children.

Password

One way to increase personal contact in the classroom is to use a password. The word may be a number, letter, new vocabulary word, question, etc. and should be changed every day. Each time the student asks the teacher for assistance the child must use the password.

In addition, each time the student leaves the classroom and returns he or she must relate the password to the *doorman* for the day. This activity is an excellent thinking stimulator and provides a vehicle for review and reinforcement of materials previously covered.

Pass-Along Pictures

Sometimes the children seem to run out of ideas, and one way to "pump" them back up is to use creative art drawing. The teacher gives each child a piece of paper and the child writes his or her name on the paper. The child then begins to draw a picture.

After a suitable time period (1 or 2 minutes), the teacher tells the children to pass their pictures to another child. The process continues for 15 or 20 minutes or until the pictures are complete. At the end of the period, the pictures are returned to the original artist. It is fun for the children to see how different their pictures are from what they originally conceived them to be.

What's in the Bag?

One way to create suspense, interest and/or develop a language or reading lesson is to hang up a large bag in the corner of the room. The bag should be stuffed with an object that will give it an odd shape or make it bulge.

The teacher should attach cards to the bag (or on an adjacent wall, bulletin board or chalkboard) on which questions are written. The children should be encouraged to read and answer the questions or to follow the direction, draw pictures, etc.

Touch Box

The teacher can collect a variety of items that illustrate textures and put them in a box. The lid to the box should have a hole cut in it large enough for a hand to be inserted and to withdraw an object, but sufficiently small that the objects are not readily seen.

A child is to reach into the box, touch an object and describe to the other children in the class how the object feels. The child then pulls the object out for the other children to inspect. The children then determine whether the description originally provided was correct or inaccurate, and in what ways.

Creative Thinking

One activity that is ideal for making use of the few spare minutes before and after a scheduled activity is to engage the children in creative problem solving. Two (or more) minds usually are better than one, and all answers, no matter how ridiculous, are acceptable. Several examples of problems to be solved are as follows:

1. How would you get a cat off a roof?
2. How would you help a schoolmate whose papers had blown away?
3. What would you do if you found $100 in the hallway?
4. What would you do if you threw a baseball through the neighbor's window?

Be a Detective

An excellent way to encourage the children to review their work and to check it for accuracy is to provide them with access to magnifying glasses. They are to use the glasses to detect errors and to see how their own work appears (neatness).

In addition, magnifying glasses may be used to assist children in maintaining their places when they read orally to the class. Finally, the teacher may use the magnifying glasses as errors are pointed out to the children during review of their work.

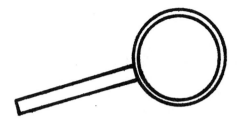

Tachistoscopic

One way to gain attention and stimulate thinking is to employ a variety of materials and styles to display words, sounds, suffixes, prefixes, etc., which the child is to learn or which are to be reviewed and reinforced. Such materials and styles also are good devices for independent activities and games.

Example:

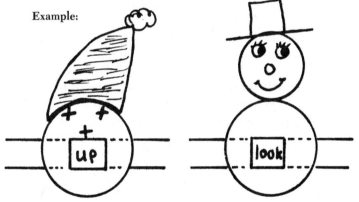

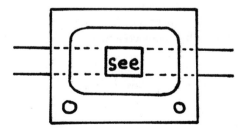

Shape and Bake

Children enjoy a tactile approach to learning. A good way to introduce, review, reinforce or just have fun with a particular sound is to bake one. If the consonant *B* is the skill for the day, then bring in the cookie dough and have the children actually shape and bake the letter *B*. When the *B* shape is done, its even more fun to eat it. *Have Fun!*

Newspapers and Magazines

The children should be permitted to put old newspapers and magazines to good use. The children should be encouraged to circle words and sounds that they know, and to cut out words and sounds that they know for use in writing stories.

Roll and Blend

To introduce the concept of blends as 2 sounds that *roll* together, the teacher might consider wearing roller skates during a particular day. The teacher should have the skates on when the children arrive at school. The letters to be emphasized during the day should be taped to the toes of the skates. This activity is a real attention-getter!

Example:

Digraph Writing

Various substances can be employed to assist in the introduction and understanding of digraphs. For example, when introducing the "wh" digraph, the children can be permitted to join in on w̲hipped cream writing. The "th" digraph permits the children to practice t̲humb writing.

In like manner, "ch" allows the children to c̲halk write and "sh" permits the children to write with s̲having cream. The children won't soon forget this experience.

Vowel Fun

Various parts of the anatomy can be used for associative purposes to introduce vowels. For example, the letter *A* is formed by using the index finger and thumb of each hand and touching the fingers and thumbs together. *E* is made by extending the index, middle and ring finger. To associate the letter *I*, the teacher points to a child's eye. *O* is emphasized by pointing to an open and very round mouth. Finally, *U* is the one vowel that permits the children to point at one another.

To introduce the long vowel sounds, the teacher should employ words that the children are particularly likely to know. To actually *perform* an activity is more illustrative.

> **Example:**   *A*—bake a cake.
>
> *E*—make a teepee.
>
> *I*—make ice cream.
>
> *O*—make a boat (from construction paper).
>
> *U*—pass around an ice cube.

Magic Glasses

An old pair of glasses (particularly 1 with the eye pieces removed) is an excellent device to gain attention. After the teacher has assembled the children (in a circle, sitting on the floor), he or she puts on the magic glasses and relates things to the children that are common knowledge to grown-ups, but that the children are not likely to realize that anyone else in the class knows.

For example, the teacher might say, "With these glasses I know everything that has happened, is happening or will ever happen." Then the teacher might say, "Last night somebody forgot to brush his or her teeth." The more drama that is built into the activity the better, and undoubtedly somebody will confess.

The teacher should strive to create the "How does she do that?" impression. Once the impression is achieved, student interest is heightened immeasurably. The promise to repeat the session later always stimulates alertness in the children.

Interest Box

Sometimes a child will lose interest in regular classroom activities and, at times, it is difficult to regain his interest with average techniques. Often by stimulating the *individual* student's interest, the teacher can increase the child's classroom participation. One way to accomplish this is to determine the child's particular likes and dislikes—what he himself likes to do with his spare time.

For example, some children particularly enjoy sports, playing cards, collecting items, space exploration, etc. To reach the individual student's interests, the teacher might consider creating an interest box oriented directly to the child's interest (i.e., hobby).

As a reward for completing regularly assigned work, the child either may attempt supplemental classroom activities or complete activities from his interest box. The special desire a child has for *his* interest will stimulate him to achieve to earn his reward.